M000308791

Outrageous Fortune

Steadfastness is a beautiful
thing, and you have it

[signature]

Book Review
in Church
Sun 9/19/21

Outrageous Fortune

Meditations on Living through a Pandemic

by
STEPHEN W. LOCKE

Foreword by Glen G. Scorgie

RESOURCE *Publications* · Eugene, Oregon

OUTRAGEOUS FORTUNE
Meditations on Living through a Pandemic

Copyright © 2021 Stephen W. Locke. All rights reserved. Except for brief quotations in critical publications or reviews, no part of this book may be reproduced in any manner without prior written permission from the publisher. Write: Permissions, Wipf and Stock Publishers, 199 W. 8th Ave., Suite 3, Eugene, OR 97401.

Resource Publications
An Imprint of Wipf and Stock Publishers
199 W. 8th Ave., Suite 3
Eugene, OR 97401

www.wipfandstock.com

PAPERBACK ISBN: 978-1-6667-0042-8
HARDCOVER ISBN: 978-1-6667-0043-5
EBOOK ISBN: 978-1-6667-0044-2

04/19/21

Unless otherwise indicated, all Scripture quotations are taken from THE MESSAGE, copyright © 1993, 2002, 2018 by Eugene H. Peterson. Used by permission of NavPress, represented by Tyndale House Publishers, a Division of Tyndale House Ministries. All rights reserved.

Scripture quotations marked (NEB) are taken from the New English Bible, copyright © Cambridge University Press and Oxford University Press 1961, 1970. All rights reserved.

Scripture quotations marked (NIV) are taken from the Holy Bible, New International Version®, NIV®. Copyright © 1973, 1978, 1984, 2011 by Biblica, Inc.™ Used by permission of Zondervan. All rights reserved worldwide. www.zondervan.com.

Scripture quotations marked (NRSV) are taken from the New Revised Standard Version Bible, copyright © 1989 National Council of the Churches of Christ in the United States of America. Used by permission. All rights reserved worldwide.

written in 2020
for the congregation of Pacific Beach Presbyterian Church

Dedication

My first dedication is to my wife, Chris,
who has supported, tempered, and encouraged me
in my education and ministry;
then to my children, Justin, Nathan, and Ashley,
who have been a delight
in their support of a father who was so visible
and who consequently made them visible.

I would also like to acknowledge my present congregation
of Pacific Beach Presbyterian Church.
They have opened their arms to my ministry among them.

Finally, I would be remiss not to mention my dear friends
Eugene and Jan Peterson,
sources of life and love to me
and now embraced by the one who gave them life.

To be, or not to be, that is the question:
Whether 'tis nobler in the mind to suffer
The slings and arrows of *outrageous fortune,*
Or to take arms against a sea of troubles
And by opposing end them?

—HAMLET, ACT III, SCENE 1

Contents

Foreword

GLEN G. SCORGIE

OUTRAGEOUS FORTUNE. AH, A phrase from William Shakespeare. Such a venerable descriptor of the maddening, monstrously unfair stuff that, well, *happens*. And keeps happening, as outrageous fortune's "slings and arrows" (and all other manner of nasty projectiles) are launched against us. Such as the current pandemic, which has robbed us of so many lives, while confining the rest of us to drastically restricted routines, and taxing our emotional health and spiritual resilience.

All of which, as Shakespeare also astutely observed, presents us with two choices going forward: to capitulate or to resist. Whenever we experience protracted suffering, we may be tempted to throw in our lot with Job's wife. Go ahead: curse God and die. She as much as says, you will have to console yourself on the slim pickings of your presumed candor and authenticity. But Stephen Locke points to a better way. In this little book, he recommends a response of godly resistance, of the kind that is able to reframe a dispiriting problem, like this awful pandemic, as strength training, as a prompt for a deeper, trusting faith. The goal becomes to flourish spiritually *despite* the circumstances—not by escaping them, but by living well in the midst of the crucible.

My friend Stephen is first and foremost a pastor. In his own words, "I can't help myself, because that is what I am." We should all esteem very highly the pastoral gift and calling, particularly when it is lived out with grace, integrity, and faithfulness. Good pastors are gifts to the church, for they mirror through their ministries the pastor-heart of the Great Shepherd himself.

Sadly, so much of the American church today is fixated on cultivating *leaders* rather than godly persons devoted to the care of souls. The cult of leadership employs no end of power words (envision, ignite, revolutionize, transform, achieve) right out of the playbook of corporate America. Much of this is only thinly veiled ambition. The truth is, we need more real, discerning, patient, empathetic pastors, whose strength flows from the core reality that they are friends of God who also care deeply about people.

Stephen Locke is such a pastor, and has been for decades. He's the real deal. Unfortunately, rather minimalist notions of the pastoral office circulate widely these days. So let me clarify that Stephen is more than *just* a pastor in that reductionist sense. He is a *pastor-theologian*, a category about which more will be said in a moment. I will simply note here, in support of my assessment, that Stephen and his wife Chris spent the better part of their honeymoon years ago studying with Francis and Edith Schaeffer at L'Abri in the Swiss Alps. He has earned a Doctor of Ministry degree, and, perhaps even more revealing, his idea of relaxing is to curl up with a good glass of wine and Karl Barth's *Church Dogmatics*, or a book by Catholic spiritual writer Henri Nouwen, or a volume of evocative poetry by Octavio Paz.

It is a special gift to be able to make big ideas and profound truths *accessible* to thoughtful readers. We already have more than enough academics who write only for an in-crowd of peers, an exclusive club of those able to follow their highly coded conversations. Unfortunately, at the other extreme, we are also inundated with so-called popular writers, many of whom seem quite willing to generate vacuous tripe and offer the thinnest of soups, simply to grab the limelight and boost sales.

But then there are those on the blessed *via media*, who are able to communicate clearly to a large thoughtful readership. They do not bury their ideas in the arcane language of the academy, nor do they "dumb down" their work because they have such low expectations—and so little real respect—for their readers. Quite the opposite!

I am happy to report that Stephen Locke belongs to this third group of communicators. An artificial division between pastors and theologians has almost ruined the church. One of the church's great needs today is for an infusion of more pastor-theologians like Stephen Locke, women and men who have true shepherd hearts fused with bright minds that have been steeped in the truths of Scripture and the traditions of the faith. Hearts and minds. Together.

The fingerprints of the late Eugene Peterson, whom Stephen Locke rightly regards as a personal mentor and friend, are all over this book. I say this not simply because so many biblical texts are quoted from *The Message* paraphrase, for which Peterson is rightly famous. I claim this because this entire volume exudes the telltale Petersonian spirit. It displays the same sure instinct to keep things real, to shepherd the people of God, and to keep redirecting their gaze ever upward, above the dispiriting chaos, to the livening and abiding Source of the Christian's strength and hope.

One might presume that anything written to address the unique challenges associated with the COVID-19 pandemic can have only a momentary relevance, a short shelf life. By implication, the publisher should hurry to get the book out, before it is consigned to the garbage pile of works that have (to echo Shakespeare again) their fleeting moment upon the stage, and then are seen no more. But the truth is that *Outrageous Fortune* was written not just to *address* the challenges faced by this pandemic. It was written *out* of the experience of the pandemic, *from* this experience. It articulates godly wisdom that could have been forged only in a fiery furnace of this magnitude. The witness of history is that our best spiritual gains are usually made in the face of difficulty and suffering. And these become enduring gains.

Outrageous Fortune consists of fifty brief meditations on texts from both the Old and New Testaments, as well as from a sprinkling of spiritual masters and literary giants through the centuries. Some readers might question the attention Locke pays here and there to non-biblical sources. After all, is not the Bible alone sufficient for every need a Christian may encounter? Well, yes and no.

One of the great rallying cries of the Reformation was *sola Scriptura*— Scripture alone. Unfortunately, some descendants of the Reformers now assume that this famous Protestant mantra means that nothing but Scripture matters. How much this blunder has cost us! And it is not what the Reformers ever intended to convey. They held that only Scripture could be the *final* arbiter of truth; it was to be the *supreme* authority for believers.

But they readily acknowledged that some of God's truth could be found in a myriad of other places as well and could and should be embraced, wherever it surfaces, as an outcome of the creator's general revelation and common grace. In fact, it is the wonderful charism of poets and sages that they can help us better see God's truth as it is mediated through the refracting lenses of their unique personalities, perceptive attentiveness, and powers of expression. Through their light, we see light. In the language of one of our old hymns, Christ shines in all that's fair.

And yet for all of that, the reader will quickly recognize that Steven Locke's imagination has been thoroughly baptized—marinated, if you will—in the truths and thought-world of the Scriptures. All the insights he gains from extra-biblical authors are filtered through this sacred lens.

Back in my college days (somewhere close to the Neanderthal age), speed reading was the rage. We paid money to take courses on how to read a whole book in five minutes, scanning each page with rapidly oscillating eyeballs, and flipping on to the next and the next with breathtaking frequency. At the time, Woody Allen bragged that he had managed to read the great Tolstoy novel *War and Peace* in one minute flat. Reflecting his comprehension level afterward, he deadpanned: "It's about Russia."

While the 1970s speed reading fad has faded, an instinctive longing to acquire and master piles of information, as quickly and efficiently as possible, persists. We think of our minds as massive storage devices. As writer Macrina Wiederkehr aptly put it, it is a radical suggestion "for us to read to be formed and transformed rather than to gather information. We are information seekers. We love to cover territory."

Stephen Locke is not offering us a treasure trove of information. He is giving us some opportunities to *meditate*—to inwardly digest, to practice the counter-intuitive discipline of inwardly digesting, of reading *slowly*. The saints of the Christian tradition have long understood that reading merely fills the mind. It is only through meditation (and, when all is said and done, finally, contemplation) that the wisdom is able to leach down from head to heart and alter the default settings of the psyche. That's really what so-called *lectio divina* is all about—leaning into a worthwhile text with all that is within us and without haste. As Stephen's mentor Eugene Peterson once explained, in such an approach to reading, "we do not take control of the text, we let the text take control of us."

Each of the meditations printed here is a spiritual commentary on a particular text. Many are drawn from Psalms, which more than any other part of Holy Scripture express the raw, unedited feelings and cries of believers struggling in the real world. But others of the meditations ruminate on powerful insights from the likes of Holocaust survivor and Nobel laureate Czeslaw Milosz, Dutch artist Vincent van Gogh, colonial-era French journalist Alexis de Tocqueville, poet Emily Dickinson, and others. If you tally them all up, you can get a pretty good sense of Stephen Locke's reading habits and what he has found soul-nourishing himself.

At one level, these meditations invite us to engage with some of the brightest minds we know. But we should not assume that this book is an indulgent feast on intellectual concepts, suspended in mid-air, detached from the grittier realities of ordinary, everyday life. No, we are constantly brought back down to earth. And these meditations are regularly punctuated with very poignant reflections. Stephen's account of how he comforted his tearful father as he died is certainly one of the most touching in the whole volume.

One great achievement of the Reformation was to wrest the Bible from the guarded clutches of a small number of Latin readers and to open it up to ordinary believers everywhere in their own languages. (It has taken Catholics a while to catch up, but since the ecumenical council of Vatican II in the 1960s, they too have been encouraging their laity to study the Bible.) But back to the Protestant timeline, it became a signature Protestant spiritual discipline to read the Scriptures privately on a daily basis in what became known as a "quiet time." Not surprisingly, a felt need eventually surfaced for assistance in drawing insights from the biblical texts. This precipitated a whole new genre of guides for the devotional reading of biblical texts. One thinks, for example, of Oswald Chambers' *My Utmost for His Highest*, Cowman's *Streams in the Desert*, or the ubiquitous *Our Daily Bread*. The best authors of such guides help us to see truths implicit in the Bible that we might otherwise have overlooked. This is what Stephen also does in the context of the unique challenges created by the current pandemic.

With the keen eye of spiritual discernment, Stephen perceives the emotional issues that have been surfacing for all of us during this seemingly endless pandemic. He understands the toll on our interior lives, a toll intensified for many by our experiences of loss and grief.

And so he has prepared these reflections on such topics as the meaning of community, finding hope in solitude, and traveling through paralysis to adventure. These were not written in a detached ivory tower, but from the context of ordinary congregational life.

While reading this book, I found myself repeatedly surprised by Stephen's ability to put his finger on emotions and inclinations I have been experiencing myself during this pandemic, like impatience, anxiety, sadness, or a strong impulse, born of misguided self-preservation, to cut myself off emotionally from needy others. It had not registered with me that others might be experiencing these same volatile waves in their own spirits. This brought to mind C. S. Lewis's observation that we read to know that we are not alone. There can be consolation even in this simple realization that our suffering is intrinsically communal. There are others who understand. Stephen Locke evidently does. Read this book with appreciation. *Slowly.*

Introduction

WHAT FOLLOWS IS A collection of meditations written during five months of the COVID-19 pandemic. I have not ordered them by theme; rather, I have simply let them stand in the sequence in which they were written to my congregation. The dates and Scriptures are all present on the pages of my musings. I desire the readers to judge for themselves where my direction and my interests were taking me along this path of spiritual healing and hardship, in the hope that all of us are on a similar path throughout this tragedy. I began writing on March 17 and ended on July 17, 2020.

At the beginning of this pandemic, I decided to take up my pen to acknowledge my own experience of this invisible enemy into my life. I wrote at least three meditations a week, hoping to expel the heartache and demons that afflicted me during this time. I also desired to write about the grace that empowered me to continue my love for congregation and God. By doing so, my interest was to provide hope to those that read them. My hope is still the same. I wish for you, reader, to take your fears, pain, love, and grace into these meditations, to judge whether these meditations have importance for your own spiritual journey. I wish for nothing else.

I do want to mention to the reader, before entering the diversity of these fifty mediations, that I have allowed my readings of philosophers, sociologists, theologians, and spiritual teachers during this pandemic to intrude upon the conversation which I have had with my congregation. They are passed on to all readers as a way of providing context for my thoughts, and hopefully the thoughts of all that are still in the fateful misfortunes of this pandemic.

My main source of inspiration has been the Psalms and the New Testament. But I have taken great pleasure in using the works of Shakespeare, Eugene Peterson, Henri J. M. Nouwen, Kierkegaard, Zygmunt Bauman, Czeslaw Milosz, T.S. Eliot, Robert Frost, Sophocles, and many others. One of the joys during this pandemic has been the time to read new and revisited works which provide a useful stimulus for my thoughts about this time.

These meditations have been a delight to write, providing a cleansing of my mind and a deepening of my understanding of the fragility of life. This *Outrageous Fortune* in which we are living is trying to define us, but I have noticed that we are trying to fight back against the tide of this erosion. Our spiritual character drives us to resist defeat. It seeks to keep alive the attributes of mercy, grace, and love. We are fighting to "be our brother's keeper."

Stephen W. Locke

January 2, 2021

Live Your Fear

March 17, 2020

Psalm 13:1–4

Long enough, God—
you've ignored me long enough.
I've looked at the back of your head
long enough. Long enough
I've carried this ton of trouble,
lived with a stomach full of pain.
Long enough my arrogant enemies
have looked down their noses at me.
Take a good look at me, God, my God;
I want to look life in the eye,
So no enemy can get the best of me
or laugh when I fall on my face.

THE TITLE OF THIS meditation is inspired by Henri J. Nouwen's wonderfully personal book *The Inner Voice of Love*. The chapter under discussion is entitled "Live Your Wounds Through." He says in this meditation, "The great challenge is *living* your wounds through, instead of *thinking* them through."[1] In this short meditation he moves through his own pain to help others connect with their inner voice, that moves from pain to love. His meditation reflects the voice of the psalms, which are expressions of lament and praise. Psalms are the expressions of our innermost self, expressing our fears, joys, loves, anxiety, hate, and the full range of our emotional life. They tell the truth. They are not necessarily elegant theology, which has been worked over through centuries of thoughtful interplay of great minds. They are raw expressions of the truth of being human, before God and the world. So, it should not surprise us when our psalmist says, "Long enough, God—you've ignored me long enough. I've looked at the back of your head long enough."

This is not only the feelings of a disgruntled believer, but a fearful individual trying to live through his fears, not being able to hear God's voice. He desires God's vindication of his feelings and an explanation of why God has turned his back on him. He wants answers, but more than that, he desires freedom from his pain and fears. He wants to live through his fears to reach the other side. He wants to get over this feeling of abandonment, to a place of peace found only in God's grace. It may be better to "live your fears" rather than trying to escape them. Honesty brings us to God's arms, allowing the fear to be embraced instead of eliminated. Living through our fear gets us to the place of understanding, instead of bypassing the education that it allows us.

The world is facing a kind of invisible fear that has the capability of removing us from a spiritual education by the lie we tell ourselves: we can manage it. In the face of this virus, this invisible fear, we can be spiritually educated only by living our fear, not trying to control it. The first step is being honest about our ability to conquer our fear, then allowing God to embrace it. We need to give into the fear, so that we can live it. By living it, we allow God to conquer it.

Václav Havel, in a letter to the world, said, "The whole of this letter is concerned, in fact, with what I really fear—the pointlessly harsh and long-lasting consequences which the present violent abuses will have for our nations."[2]

While this letter was about his present political situation in the 70s and the long-lasting effects of violence in Czechoslovakia, his fear can be transferred to ours. I, too, fear the long-lasting effects of this virus, like

---

1. Nouwen, *Inner Voice*, 109.
2. Havel, *Art of the Impossible*, 53.

Havel feared the long-lasting effects of violence in his country. That is why we must live our fears, now. Bring them under the tutelage of God for our edification and education, into a greater spiritual peace.

Where Are You Looking?

March 19, 2020

Psalm 121:1-2

I look up to the mountains;
does my strength come from mountains?
No, my strength comes from God,
who made heaven, and earth, and mountains.

MOST OF THE TIME when we fall prey to the temptations toward destructive thoughts and deeds, it is because of where our eyes take us. Our eyes are what transport our thoughts, turning them to dangerous temptations, arising from desires of what Paul calls the flesh. It then turns them into actions, that find us in places we should not be. In a similar respect, our eyes are the instruments that raise our fears and doubts. When we step into a plane, then watch it take off, there is always a bit of fear that moves through us. We see ourselves flying up in the air with nothing underneath us, realizing that we are dangling in the wind. Not until we get up in the clouds, where we cannot see the ground, do we start to feel at ease.

Several years ago, I took a trip to Ireland where I traveled to the Cliffs of Moher. Back then, you were able to walk to the edge of a cliff that had no railing and look down. Not wanting to appear a coward among my friends, I walked close to the edge and began to see the bottom as I walked closer, then my legs turned to jelly. Still not wanting to give up, I crawled to the edge, looked down, and felt paralyzed. I slowly crawled backward, feeling the power come back into my legs, turned around, and felt relieved. My eyes saw the hills behind me, which gave me comfort.

Our eyes control much of what we feel, what we want, and what we need. The psalmist understands this basic human function. When he says, "I look up to the mountains; does my strength come from mountains," he is expressing two perspectives of what mountains provide. First, for someone who is on a pilgrimage, who needs to go over those hills, the mountains represent an obstacle that needs to be overcome. Secondly, they represent a place where God was most alive in Israel. Some of the most important events in Israel's life happened when those that traveled up to the mountains created a memory and way of life for the nation—Moses and the law, Abraham and Isaac.

When the pilgrims on their way to Jerusalem—the pilgrims who are represented in this psalm—saw the mountains, these two thoughts were at work in their consciousness. It all depended on what glasses they were wearing with which to see the mountains. Were they wearing the fearful and tired glasses, or were they wearing the glasses ground from faith? The first pair of glasses creates despair and drudgery. The second pair of glasses creates a spiritual joy that propels them over the mountain with memories of stories that define the history of their people. Above all, they are excited about a God who has given them strength and energy throughout their life and the life of Israel.

So, the question is where are you looking, or, more importantly, who are you looking for? The eyes of your heart will lead you to what you desire. *In this time of self-quarantine, turn your eyes to the mountains and beyond to the one who defines your faith and your very existence.*

Developing Good Habits

March 22, 2020

The spiritual life is not a life before, after, or beyond our everyday existence.

No, the spiritual life can only be real when it is lived

in the midst of the pains and joys of here and now.

Therefore, we need to begin with a careful look

at the way we think, speak, feel and act

from hour to hour, day to day, week to week, and year to year,

in order to become more fully aware of our hunger for the Spirit.

—Henri J. M. Nouwen[1]

One of the hardest disciplines to develop in our life is to stay in the moment. We all have inquisitive minds that turn us to what is going to happen or what is happening somewhere else, other than in our own lives. When we are distracted by our inquisitive mind, most of the time we are obsessed with fear and anxiety. When that happens, we begin to think negatively about the world and even our life. The only way to come out from under the unpredictable nature of things is to embrace the moment and allow the Spirit to plant us into this very place where we stand. But this is not easy. Jesus knew this as well. That is why he said the following after a long teaching segment on faith: "So do not be anxious about tomorrow; tomorrow will look after itself. Each day has trouble enough of its own" (Matt 6:34). This, without question, is the truth, and cannot be altered. Therefore, embrace

---

1. Nouwen, *Inner Voice*, 40.

today, the here and now, *allowing your spirit to wander in God's playground of peace.*

Today is Sunday. I am finding it strange to embrace this day, because I should be with all of you; worshiping and talking about the ministry and our lives, also talking about the mysteries of life that keep us adventurous. Like all of you, I must develop new habits during this uncertain time of isolation. I have decided that to help me stay in the moment I am going to read, write, and take walks with my wife and dog. To enjoy all this is enough. But I must confess it is hard to say that, because I am so used to working with others to get things done. I must confess that it is hard for me to develop disciplined habits. My character pushes me to be obsessive more than disciplined. So, when I sit down to read, the stack of books by my side begins to get larger, until I just have to stop. My discipline is to just keep going, until I am exhausted. It is a hard thing to admit that I need the restraint of others. I am so pleased that God takes the time to gently say to me: rest, rest. Over the years, I have learned to live with this flaw, because to depend upon time schedules and lists simply has not worked. Yet, I find myself strangely at peace today, embracing the moment. Letting tomorrow take care of itself, because there will be enough to deal with, when the time comes.

The trick in life is to find your own way, with God, through the every-day moments of your life. How you develop your way with God is singular. How we develop our life with God, as a church, is collective. Love what you find in the moment with God, and you will find rest and refreshment. I find this refreshment and rest with God, in the tramping out of words on a page, trying to say to all of you something worthwhile. I will keep doing this every day, in the here and now, because it is also keeping me in the here and now with God.

I like to think when I do these things that it brings me peace and happiness and that these will spill over into my life with others. It is incumbent upon us to find that which gives us pleasure and feeds our spirit. We can find this only in the moment, in the day, this day, which has everything in it to bring us closer to God. Don't worry about tomorrow, instead *allow your spirit to wander in God's playground of peace.* It is there that our hunger for meaning and for a delightful place with God will find its purpose.

Home

March 24, 2020

John 14:1–4

Home is where you are truly safe.

It is where you can receive what you desire.

You need human hands to hold you there so you don't run away again.

But when you come home and stay home,

you will find the love that will bring rest to your heart.

—HENRI J. M. NOUWEN[1]

JESUS LOVED THE IMAGE of home, as we learn from the gospel of John. Just before Jesus was to suffer the humiliation of a trial and execution, he used the word "home" to comfort his disciples upon his impending death. He said, "Let not your hearts be troubled. Believe in God, believe also in me. In my father's home are many rooms. If I go away, I will bring you to where I am" (John 14:1–2). His words pulled them into a picture of what heaven is like; it is where Jesus is. It is home. Heaven is not some cloudy place filled with angels, cherubim, and seraphim. It is a home, simple in nature, with Jesus always at the head of the table. In other words, heaven is now, and was, and always will be—because God is now, and was, and always will be.

---

1. Nouwen, *Inner Voice*, 30.

Home is a comforting symbol because it expresses a feeling we remember. But in our present situation, we may feel the walls closing in on us. Home is now a place to which we are bound, because the world is not safe. It is not filled with the joy and ease of a nice lunch, or a meaningful conversation with friends across the table. Home is now a place to which we must escape, in order to make ourselves and the world safe. We know this is temporary. But we have no clue when it is going to end, so it robs us of the feeling of peace and hope.

In this time in our life together as a human community, Jesus wants to say to all of us, "Come home and stay home, with me, and I will give you rest." To find this rest, our task is to keep our eyes on the beauty Jesus provides us, with each other and our connection to creation. It may be a flower, a piece of music, a picture, a conversation with a spouse or friend, or, of course, reading familiar Scriptures that stir the imagination towards a vision of God. It is also time to develop a routine that is not oppressive but freeing. You might want to make phone calls to friends, go outside for a brief walk, read a new book, work in the yard, or just silently enjoy the solitude which God fills up with the sounds of love and peace.

But the one thing we can't afford to do is to see our homes as a place of isolation and loneliness. Therefore, we do need to make every effort to reach out in any way we can, within the safety guidelines to others, which then turns our homes into a place where we can feel connected. I am reminded of a sentence by Wendel Berry, the essayist, novelist, and small farm owner: "[B]y ourselves we have no meaning and no dignity; by ourselves we are outside the human definition, outside our own identity."[2] His point is clear and true. We can only be ourselves, that is, the collective body of humanity, if we still see ourselves as part of the world. Therefore, keep up your connections, while finding your solitude. The virus might rob us of our freedom to live as before, but it cannot rob us of who we are.

2. Berry, *Home Economics*, 184.

Breathing in God

March 26, 2020

Genesis 2:7–8 (NIV)

Then the Lord God formed man from the dust of the ground, and breathed into his nostrils the breath of life; and the man became a living being.

ONE OF MY FAVORITE old hymns is "Breathe on Me, Breath of God." Its words are simple and pure, as well as providing us with a meditative symbol of growing with God. The first line reads:

> Breathe on me, Breath of God,
> fill me with life anew,
> that I may love the way you love,
> and do what you would do.

The songwriter takes us back to Genesis 2, when God breathed the breath of life into the human being he created. As the imagination of the songwriter wanders through the creation, he experiences the love of God. As God breathes life into the human being, he imagines that it is love that is flowing from God to this cherished created being. It is not just existence but the very essence of God that is being poured into the human, who is now a part of God. Adam is a spiritual being and not just an animal that lives with instincts. Adam and Eve are reflective beings with the very thoughts and essence of God, who fills them up with his very essence.

The songwriter interprets this action of God as the creation of a spiritual way of life. The act of breathing is a reminder that we are endowed and entrusted with God's essence that is to be lived out in the world, which is also created by God. Breathing is a refreshing and necessary part of our life with God. It is not mechanical but spiritual. When we breathe we are to imagine that we are breathing in God—God's spiritual way of life. This breathing in of God is connected to the heart, which is cleansed when we imagine that it is God's breath entering our tired and painful body. Breathing in God means we are not alone, nor are we alone in the world with others, who are breathing in the breath of God alongside all those we love.

The unfortunate result of our invisible enemy is that it increases our fear of breathing. We are afraid of breathing in the air around us, fearing the virus may enter the sacred place of our God-given life. Air is now suspect, and breathing is now harmful, instead of a sacred act of rest and assurance. Breathing has lost its sacredness of peace and knowledge. But only if we let it. If we do, it is not the air that is our enemy, it is fear. Find a way to breathe in God, or better yet find a *place* to breathe in God. It is our way of fighting against this enemy. It is our way of accepting the gift of God's life for us.

In the months ahead of us, we are going to engage in a lot of sitting. That means our minds will tend to wander off to worry about our economic life, our physical life, our family's well-being, and many other distracting images. It might be the time to reconnect with God in a new way. Concentrate on your breathing, and imagine that you are breathing in God and, with God, a new life for the world. It might be unusual to say, but breathing has a spiritual content to it. In fact, there is spiritual thinking going on as we breathe. So I suggest, listen to your breathing, think your breathing, and fill yourself up with the love of God. Then let your mind wander back to creation and the Genesis story to find a new connection and a renewal of spirit.

Stay well, stay safe, and let God renew you.

Responsibility in
an Age of Individualism

May 27, 2020

Genesis 4:8–10 (NIV)

Cain said to his brother Abel, "Let us go out to the field." And when they were in the field, Cain rose up against his brother Abel and killed him. Then the Lord said to Cain, "Where is your brother Abel?" He said, "I do not know; am I my brother's keeper?

SINCE THE 1950S AND 60s there has been a diligent pursuit of individualism that has somewhat characterized our country. But as we know from Tocqueville and others, this characteristic was forged into the American experience from the very beginning and also in most of the Western world. It is part of our nature, you might say. But while there has been a pursuit of individualism, there has also been a sense of responsibility grafted onto this singular pursuit. When the balance is tilted to individualism, society begins to divide itself towards the extremes of both those necessary political viewpoints that make for a vibrant culture. Today, during the reign of this invisible enemy, we see these divisions in striking contrast. We see it played out on television and in the op-ed sections of our newspapers and magazines.

As I witness this dance of our two national characteristics, it is my opinion that we have slipped more towards individualism than the use of our freedom to engage the necessary action of responsibility to society and others. Now, of course, this opinion may be because of my own proclivity to advance the cause to be "my brother's keeper," rather than looking after number one. But when I see people in the streets protesting the decisions of those that are trying to be responsible for others' lives, I get worried that the balance between the two is being heavily weighted toward individualism. This inhibits any discussion of facts or common sense that could breathe a more respectful air of decency among us. There may be a time to have a spirited debate, but this does not seem to be the time to enter protest or resistance against those who are trying to be responsible agents for others, especially the less fortunate.

Christianity can be an instructive voice in this conflict. In fact, philosophers and sociologists around the world have said that religion has much to teach us during this time. Jacques Derrida, a French philosopher, has said, "Religion presumes access to the responsibility of a free self.... Religion is responsibility or it is nothing at all."[1] He came to this conclusion not through an analysis of all religion but from the head of Christianity, Jesus. He saw Jesus as a leader who took responsibility for the lives of others. The most dramatic image of this responsibility is the cross. This, he suggests, is the heart of all religious practice, whether it is performed as a Christian or a Buddhist.

In like manner, Paul shows this same responsibility for his church and all the Christians in the known world at that time, when he says, "As it is written, 'For your sake we are being killed all day long, we are accounted as sheep to be slaughtered'" (Rom 8:36 NRSV). He understands that Christian responsibility is enduring hardship and frustration for the sake of the other, even at the price of our life. This is the heart of his Christian practice. His desire is to follow Jesus, even to the cross. This kind of responsibility is how the world is healed and brought together out of a love for the purposes of God's Kingdom. Even though there is a certain horror attached to this responsibility, giving your life to the other, there is a certain beauty that lives on for the world to mimic. I end this little meditation with a quote from Jan Patočka, a Czech Philosopher, "Because of its foundation within the abyssal profundity of the soul, Christianity represents to this day the most powerful means—never yet superseded but not yet thought through either—by which mankind is able to struggle against his own decline."[2]

---

1. Derrida, *Gift of Death*, 67.
2. Patočka, *Heretical Essays*, 108.

Free as a Bird

May 28, 2020

Psalm 124:6–8

Oh, blessed be God!
He didn't go off and leave us.
He didn't abandon us defenseless,
helpless as a rabbit in a pack of snarling dogs.
We've flown free from their fangs,
free of their traps, free as a bird.
Their grip is broken;
we're free as a bird in flight.
God's strong name is our help,
the same God who made heaven and earth.

WHENCE COMES OUR TROUBLE? What is the trouble that we experience? There are so many ways that we could answer these questions. Our trouble comes from the hazards of the earth, from the world of nature and earthly powers. But our trouble also comes from relationships and our own undoing. Trouble also comes through spiritual realities and responsibilities that we neglect. Who has not experienced the trauma of guilt that has paralyzed us, as we try to put the pieces of our life together? Trouble is everywhere. It is in temptation, love, desires, and the weaknesses that exist in all of us.

But even though we feel defenseless against many of our troubles, we have a God whose strengths are no match for the trouble that meets us every day. We can fly up, free as a bird, as dangers begin to surmount, then fly back down with God to engage the trouble we fill powerless to fight.

It is common for us to question ourselves and God when various troubles affect our lives with pain. I remember my father turning to me in the last months of his life battling cancer and asking me, "What did I do to deserve this?" I saw the longing in his eyes as he asked me. Being a pastor, I know he thought I had the secrets to all the mysteries of life, including the reason for the pain he was enduring. I turned to him and said, "You did nothing, Dad, to deserve this. Nobody deserves this. The world is a cruel place, sometimes. You just happened to be in the way when the world decided to dish out some of its pain. But I am here, and so is God." My dad never cried before, but at that moment the tears that had been pressurized for years erupted with love and sadness. I never felt as close to him than at that moment or in the next few months before his death. Sometimes help means saying the truth, instead of trying to find a clever or profound answer that, in the end, is just conjecture or a lie. To this day, I believe he appreciated my honesty, which translated into love for me and maybe even himself.

Help comes from the strangest places, but always from God. God knows how to help, not just to eradicate pain. Help means standing with people as they struggle with their fear; it means trembling in the thought that we know nothing about the suffering of the world, but decide to shake our fist at it and then bow to its inevitability. It also means relaxing, as we experience God putting us on the back of a bird to fly above the dangers below. Help can mean so many different things for us, but only God knows us and knows what help means in our situation. Most of the time it boils down to this: compassion and honesty. There are no greater healing agents. Honesty gives us a chance to evaluate our life of trouble without the need of inventing strange conclusions about our problem. Compassion helps us stand in the center of the trouble without fear, knowing that others hurt with us. Of course, this is God's wisdom and love for us. God's strength is in God's truth. We cannot run away from God's truth. It is better to run to it. We may be surprised at what we find.

Laughing until We Change

March 30, 2020

After two weeks of being confined, listening to the news, calling my kids, and doing chores, it is time for a change. Maybe it's time to laugh. Look around, watch all the funny behavior of people and the funny things people say. It is delightful at times just to be able to laugh at the world, ourselves, and even God. In an interview with the BBC, John Cleese, creator of *A Fish Called Wanda* and *Fawlty Towers* said, "One the things I really like to do is laugh. Big fat belly laughs. It is like cleansing the soul." But the thing about laughter is you have to look for it, you have to want it. If you can't laugh at something funny, it means you are so locked up in yourself and the situation that the button that releases the curtain over the funny bone is stuck. If so, it needs to be dislodged, loosened up, so laughter can once again escape from your heart.

What I do, when I need a change, is watch my DVDs of *Fawlty Towers* and *Father Ted*. Both are based on the old comedy style called "farce." Both of these shows have characters that are outlandish, with over-the-top performances that portray behaviors most people would never do. But when the characters do, it makes us feel so good; it is farcical. It is cathartic, while allowing us to see the world differently. In *Fawlty Towers*, Basil, the husband, is so afraid of Sybil, his wife, that it is hilarious when he finally has had enough and begins to yell at her. He finally gets the courage to stand up for himself. What is funny about this is that he does it so badly and that Sybil seems so unaffected by it all. She sees right through the tortured words. She just stands there with an indifferent smile, fully knowing that she will be in control in the next minute. Sound familiar? When the scene finishes, it is just time to laugh at yourself.

It might be hard to picture Jesus laughing, but he must have. In fact, some of the stories he tells and things he says, if taken in a certain way, are just funny. The one I like is the story of the rich fool (Luke 12:13–21 NRSV). The parable reads, "The land of a rich man produced abundantly. And he thought to himself, 'What should I do, for I have no place to store my crops?' Then he said, 'I will do this: I will pull down my barns and build larger ones, and there I will store all my grain and my goods. And I will say to my soul, Soul, you have ample goods laid up for many years; relax, eat, drink, be merry.' But God said to him, 'You fool! This very night your life is being demanded of you. And the things you have prepared, whose will they be?' So it is with those who store up treasures for themselves but are not rich toward God." I don't know why, but whenever I read this story, it makes me laugh. How crazy to think that you can stash your money in a barn, retreat to your house, and you will be happy. It is hilarious. Why? Because many of us would think or even do the same. We equate happiness with security. Jesus exposes this and all our musings as idiotic dreams and calls them folly. I love this. Besides, I picture Jesus, after telling this parable, engaging in a little chuckle.

Laughing at ourselves is an important thing to do. I laugh at myself every time I try to fix my computer. If I didn't, I would go mad. So, laugh at others, yourself, and even God. It is not beyond God to do some funny things. Laugh until you change. Just remember that God is most likely laughing at us, too. He probably can't wait to give us a list of all the things we did that gave him a good laugh.

Remain Anchored in Your Community

March 31, 2020

Romans 12:11–13

Don't burn out; keep yourselves fueled and aflame.
    Be alert servants of the Master,
cheerfully expectant.
Don't quit in hard times; pray all the harder.
Help needy Christians; be inventive in hospitality.

PAUL, LIKE ALL OF us, counted on the hospitality of our Christian community to get him through hard times. It is like a lifeline at times. We can always count on it being there for us, when we are sinking. But we can also be a lifeline for others as well. Mutuality is what sustains community. It is never one-sided. The needs and pain of others are not just disseminated to a portion of the population; they fall upon all of us at different times. That is why we need to look at our own pain, as well as the pain of others. Paul commands us to help needy Christians, from all walks of life, who need the kindness of God. It is this attachment and kindness that creates oneness and unity.

Henri J.M. Nouwen, no stranger to pain and the healing of others, says, "It is important to remain as much in touch as possible with those who know you, love you, and will protect you . . . . Think about your community as holding a long line that girds your waist. Your community can pull you back when its members see that you are forgetting why you were sent (out by God)."[1] In this kind of community, where everyone understands they are a lifeline for others, we can feel safe and loved. That is what we can do for others in this time of need, as the invisible enemy still lurks in the shadows of our world.

We are called to remain anchored to our community in this time of isolation by phone, letters, emails, and cards. We still have the means to connect with one another and distribute what Paul calls "practicing hospitality" (Rom 12:13). With the command to be hospitable there comes a necessary determination of the community, to be responsible. In fact, to be hospitable is to be responsible. It means you have determined that everyone in your community is your responsibility. When this is accepted as the rule, then everyone has a lifeline. There is no one person that stands outside this responsibility. It is not that there is a perfect equity of action; there is always a sacrificial nature to our responsibility. When this is understood, there is a sense of embrace and love that transcends our own pain.

By holding on to this responsibility as an ethical and spiritual action, we hold on to the hope that we are contributing to the betterment of all things in the world. In this time of trouble, we have the chance to show our community that we love them, through the nature of our hospitality in Christ. As I am writing this, I am thinking of many of you whom I will be calling. This is not just my obligation; it is my privilege to be connected to you. Being connected to each other is like being connected by our pain and joy. Suffering with others is not all distasteful. I can sometimes be the only thing that helps us hang on to what makes us human.

Stay well, stay safe, and pray always.

---

1. Nouwen, *Inner Voice*, 61.

Standing Near Our Grace

April 2, 2020

Mark 10:32 (NEB)

They were on the way, going up to Jerusalem. Jesus was going ahead of them, and they were amazed, but those who followed were afraid. He took the twelve aside again and began to tell them what was going to happen to him.

As WE COME CLOSE to Palm Sunday, Mark draws our attention to the community of Jesus on the way to Jerusalem to face their future, which looked grim. There is little doubt that Jesus brought with him a rather large entourage of people whom he had been teaching and who were on the way with him to celebrate the Passover. When they were coming closer to Jerusalem, Mark writes about a very curious event between Jesus and his disciples. It seems that his chosen disciples were next to him on the road, while the other followers were a ways back. According to the context, Jesus was talking about what was going to happen to him when he entered Jerusalem. Then Mark writes, "Jesus was going ahead of them [the disciples] and they were amazed [astonished], but those who followed [further behind] were afraid." It would seem odd that Mark directs our attention to such an event. It seems strange that he would tell us the details of the feelings of the followers and disciples on their way to Jerusalem. So, I take it to be a significant opportunity for Mark to teach us something. But what?

Let's look at this through spiritual eyes. Those that were closer to Jesus, who were more sophisticated about what he taught and experienced his grace, were not afraid. Furthermore, they were more aware of his astonishing poise in telling them about his death. They were surrounded by his spiritual grace, which gave them the power to face his death and maybe even their own. Facing an uncertain future can be terrifying. But the closer we are to our strength, which holds the future, we find ourselves looking forward to what tomorrow might bring. The followers who were far behind Jesus on his way to Jerusalem were afraid, because they were not privileged to be raised up by his spiritual poise. They were afraid, because they had not been privy to the demeanor and the words of Jesus. They were excluded from such confidence and surety of purpose.

The more we come closer to Jesus, who is our grace and strength, the more we feel confident to face the future. Walking close to Jesus is like walking toward a fire in complete fire gear. You can go into a fire, confident and prepared, while being ready to help those around you. The disciples can walk into the fire of Jerusalem because they have their fire gear on. They are protected by truth and grace, knowing that Jesus's purpose has now become theirs. They now have the instruments and skill to maneuver through their life, to bring the kingdom of God to the world. They will need more training for this, however. We, too, are in need of more training. All it takes is standing next to our grace, listening to the words of truth that bring a poise to our life. It means racing to the front, not standing back trying to escape the hard words of Jesus. It means being able to face your fears, through the power of love given to us by the lover of humanity. If this were not so, we would all go mad. Somewhere, in all of us, is the hope that we are connected to something greater than we are—and that thing is love.

How Much Can We Take?

April 7, 2020

Galatians 6:2 (NIV)

Bear one another's burdens, and in this way,
you will fulfill the law of Christ.

PAUL SEEMS TO INDICATE in Galatians, and other places as well, that sacrificial love and bearing each other's burdens is the purpose of the law. If we engage in these activities, we will please God and live out the purpose of God for this world, thus benefiting humanity, which is the purpose of God. But the question we always ask ourselves is "How much can we take?" We are letting so much pain into our lives. Is it worth it to enter into this sacrificial existence? If we have children, they need us; if we are in high school, we have friends who need us. How much can we let others' pain intrude into our world without losing our buoyancy? Of course, there is no way to measure this question, which means there is no way to find an answer that fits all. What might help us understand what Paul and Jesus are driving at is to try is understand what it means to carry each other's burdens, through the context of living the cross.

A story that has always helped me understand what it means to carry burdens and to heal the brokenness of others is found in a rabbinic story that has come to be known as "The Wounded Healer." The story goes something like this:

"A young Rabbi who wished to know when the Messiah would come went to ask his teacher this question. His teacher in turn told him to go to a cave outside the city and talk to the prophet who lives there. So, the young Rabbi went and asked his pressing question to him. The prophet told him, 'Why don't you go ask him yourself.' But the young Rabbi asked the prophet, 'How shall I know him?' The prophet said the Messiah is the one sitting in the gate of the city, sitting among the wounded, binding his own wounds one at a time, in order to be ready to help someone else when they needed him.' So, the young Rabbi went out to find the Messiah, and when he did, sat down among the wounded and began to bind his own wounds, one at a time."[1]

There are several important observations in this story that I believe help us understand how to carry each other's burdens. First, the Messiah is always among us, ready to help us heal from the spiritual damage to our life. Second, the Messiah's example helps us prepare to help others in times of need. His example and his wisdom in knowing how to heal our wounds helps us carry burdens, without being destroyed ourselves. Finally, it is essential that the Messiah's wisdom, and ours as well, comes by healing our own wounds. Healing ourselves is essential to knowing how to carry the burdens of others. Unless we know what we need, after a deep wound has injured us, it is difficult to know how to help others—especially when you think of the spiritual wounds that we incur all the time.

Jesus, Paul, or Peter do not ask us to destroy ourselves in the pursuit of sacrificial love. They ask only that we let Jesus, the Messiah, heal us and to know that even the Messiah needed to take the time to bind his wounds. Knowing how to do this—or, I should say, knowing how to let the Messiah do this—is the wisdom we need to be the best healer of spiritual devastation. The Messiah is the Wounded Healer, and we can be, too. Bind your spiritual burdens that have become infected, one at a time, allowing God to become the healing salve of your heart. Then we will know how much we can take, and how God can be the new measure of our ability to carry the burdens of others.

1. Nouwen, *Wounded Healer*, 81–82.

Bring Patience to Your Troubles

April 13, 2020

John 11:1–6

A man was sick, Lazarus of Bethany, the town of Mary and her sister Martha. This was the same Mary who massaged the Lord's feet with aromatic oils and then wiped them with her hair. It was her brother Lazarus who was sick. So, the sisters sent word to Jesus, "Master, the one you love so very much is sick."

When Jesus got the message, he said, "This sickness is not fatal. It will become an occasion to show God's glory by glorifying God's Son." Jesus loved Martha and her sister and Lazarus, but oddly, when he heard that Lazarus was sick, he stayed on where he was for two more days. After the two days, he said to his disciples, "Let's go back to Judea."

THIS TRULY IS ONE of the most touching stories in Jesus's life. His actions show his deep love for Lazarus's family, all the while stretching their friendship by demanding their patience in the midst of a tragic event. The story goes like this. Jesus is in Bethany, weeks before he enters Jerusalem. He stays with Lazarus and his family, who showed him great hospitality and friendship. Jesus decides to get away before the coming days, which will be filled with sorry and pain. He knows that Lazarus is sick when he leaves. While he is gone, he gets word from Bethany that Lazarus is close to death. But, instead of getting up immediately to return, he waits two days. This must have seemed like an eternity for Lazarus's sisters, who had seen Jesus do many miracles and were hoping for one for Lazarus. But it didn't come. Lazarus died while Jesus was waiting to come back.

When Jesus returned, Lazarus had been four days in the grave already. As you might expect, he was not warmly greeted. Martha, one of the sisters, was quick to blame Jesus for her brother's death. Her actions were motivated by grief, anger, and an impulsiveness driven by her disgust with Jesus. She knew that Jesus could do anything, but she wouldn't allow herself to be patient enough to see it. She had buried her patience with her brother and her grief. Many of us do the same thing. We want something to happen so much, and immediately, that we throw out our patience with our anger. But when we are dealing with God in faith and love, we have to learn patience, or we are going to be angry much of the time.

Whenever I think of this story, I turn again to Henri J.M. Nouwen, who writes in a little devotion called "Live Patiently with the 'Not Yet'" the following: "Be patient. When you feel lonely, stay with your loneliness. Avoid the temptation to let your fearful self run off. Let it teach you its wisdom; let it tell you that you can live instead of just surviving. Gradually you will become one, and you will find that Jesus is living in your heart and offering you all you need."[1]

I believe the last line sums up how to develop patience. When we understand that Jesus offers us all we need, learning patience becomes a clearer path to handle the troubles of life. How many times have we flown-off-the-handle and said mean things because we have formulated in ourselves that things could have been different, if others just cared? In the story of Jesus and Lazarus, Jesus cared. But little of that mattered to Lazarus's family and friends. Impatience strips our belief in each other. Love and forgiveness restore it. That is where the story ends. But the question of what happened still remains. It still remains with us as well. More than anything during the raid of this invisible enemy, we need patience to endure the long and winding road we are on.

1. Nouwen, *Inner Voice*, 49–50.

Community Feel

April 13, 2020

Words have meanings: some words, however, also have a "feel."
The word "community" is one of them. It feels good:
whatever the word community may mean, it is good "to have a community,"
"to be a community."

—Zygmunt Bauman[1]

Dr. Bauman is right when he says that there are words that have more of a feel to them than an exact meaning. "Community" is definitely one of those words. No matter how hard sociologists try to define community, the word is always running away from them. It is different from the word "institution" or even "church." Both of those entities are defined by what they operationally contain, in order to use those labels. Institutions have structure, order, rules, tradition, hierarchy, and a place within the way of life of a nation. Even the word church has many of the traits we find in institutional structures. But when we use the word "community" to say who we are or to whom we belong, hardly any of those characteristics attach themselves to what we mean. Community is hard to nail down; that is because we feel it more than understand it through a rational process of our sociological tools. We cannot dissect what a community is, like we can a governmental institution. We feel what a community is. It is warm, cozy, a shelter amid the storm. It has rules, but there seem to be only two: love and be responsible. Against such, there can be no rules that when added make it clearer. Those two verbs say it all.

1. Bauman, *Community*, 1.

When Paul talks about the church in his letters, I believe he has in mind the feeling of community, not the rules of the institution. He is more concerned about our behavior toward others, not the rules that are used to judge others or to meticulously follow to maintain the peace. Peace is maintained in a more organic way through the common features of hospitality, care, love, and responsibility. In his letter to the Romans, in 13:7–10, he writes, "Owe no one anything, except to love one another; for the one who loves another has fulfilled the law. The commandments, 'You shall not commit adultery; You shall not murder; You shall not steal; You shall not covet'; and any other commandment, are summed up in this word, 'Love your neighbor as yourself.' Love does no wrong to a neighbor; therefore, love is the fulfilling of the law" (NIV). Love has a feel to it, just like the word community. Paul wants those who follow Jesus to have a feel about them—the feeling of love, care, embrace, and unity. These are created in the community of faith by a deeply held respect for each other and a responsible spirit of love for those who belong. This is how our communities are maintained.

Another feeling of community is captured in the word freedom. One of our most brilliant scholars of the previous generation was F.F. Bruce. So sure was he that Paul saw his pastoral role as a preacher of freedom that he entitled his last book *Paul: Apostle of the Heart Set Free*. He believed that Paul's role, at heart, was to build communities that reflected the kind of feel that Jesus had with his disciples, a feeling of love and freedom, that was guided by the spirit of Christ, not by the political structures of the temple. Jesus was more about teaching his disciples the dynamics of freedom rather than the mechanics of institutions. One is more like a community, the other like a political structure. While the church has veered off this road throughout the years, the one thing that it longs for is community. That feeling of belonging cannot be created by structures that maintain institutions. There are no formulas, gimmicks, or books that can establish the communities we long for. Only the two verbs that flow from a heart ablaze for Jesus: love and be responsible.

In this season of isolation, these two verbs are possibly more important to us than before we were restricted. Isolation breeds feelings of despair because we cannot be around the people who help us understand community. It also breeds blame, which helps no one. But we can grow our hearts into something better by keeping in touch with one another, and we can continue to pray for one another. These are the acts that connect us and provide the feeling that comes from that sacred and beautiful word "community."

Acknowledging Your Powerlessness

April 15, 2020

Genesis 22:1–4 (NRSV)

After these things God tested Abraham. He said to him, "Abraham!" And he said, "Here I am." He said, "Take your son, your only son Isaac, whom you love, and go to the land of Moriah, and offer him there as a burnt offering on one of the mountains that I shall show you." So Abraham rose early in the morning, saddled his donkey, and took two of his young men with him, and his son Isaac; he cut the wood for the burnt offering, and set out and went to the place in the distance that God had shown him. On the third day Abraham looked up and saw the place far away.

EVERYONE HAS EXPERIENCED THEIR own powerlessness in demanding situations, in which we are thrust into doing something hard, without any experience or skill. When I was in high school, my football coach, who was also the track coach, talked me into running the four hundred-yard sprint, when someone else couldn't run. I told him that I couldn't do it, because I hadn't had the training to pace myself. I usually like sprints. Longer runs were not my thing. I proved him right; I came in last. I disappointed him and myself. It was humiliating on every level. I realized how powerless I was over my body and my will to push ahead. I realized that life is often more difficult than I had imagined. It places obstacles and challenges before us.

Unless we take them, we don't know how powerless we are; knowing our powerlessness is a good thing.

Abraham had a challenge before him, and he wondered if he could rise to the occasion. The sacrificing of his son at God's request must have beaten him down to the point that he realized he couldn't do it. The only way to do it was to trust in God and his own powerlessness. For unless he acknowledged he couldn't do it, he could never have completed the task. This is the mystery of faith: it is first powerlessness before it has the ability to create the power to trust. Once we begin to trust, we can begin to live for God, in the freedom of our powerlessness. "Your willingness to let go of your desire to control your life reveals a certain trust. The more you relinquish your stubborn need to maintain power, the more you will get in touch with the One who has the power to heal and guide you."[1]

Throughout his life, Abraham tried to short-circuit the power of faith for the power of control. In times of deep distress, he fell back on this old habit, developed through his years of building his little kingdom in Assyria. It was not easy for him to acknowledge his powerlessness, given his place among the people who became his company. But at a certain moment, when his whole life was on the line, he felt to his knees and trembled and acknowledged his inability to face his task. Only then was he able to face this daunting future, which demanded faith and not heroics.

My guess is that his way to the mountain where his son would be sacrificed might have been bearable, given that he had time before having to act on God's challenging demand. But when he saw the mountain on the third day, his heart must have sunk. It was coming upon him very soon. This is when he must have had a crisis; who wouldn't? He saw his son. He prayed to God and fell to the ground. "Lord, help," are the only words he (or we) could utter at that moment. It was just then that the powerlessness of human power was acknowledged as his hope. Walking up the mountain, he took his weakness to the very top. Then, it happened. The power of faith, the faith learned in his powerlessness, took over, and it gave him the tenacity and courage to continue. It is this faith in which we live today. It is the faith of Jesus walking to the cross, the faith of Abraham walking up the mountain, both coming to grips with the weakness of their flesh and their will, born out of the acknowledgment of human frailty, but overcoming it in the power of faith.

1. Nouwen, *Inner Voice*, 109.

Hope in Silence

April 15, 2020

If there is no God,
Not everything is permitted to man.
He is still his brother's keeper
And he is not permitted to sadden his brother,
By saying there is no God.

—CZESLAW MILOSZ[1]

THERE IS NO QUESTION that the Bible is a book of hope. We have Jürgen Moltmann to thank for reminding us of this fact. It establishes the story of God through images and prophetic visions that pull the future into the present. We are then asked to believe this future and, at the same time, live as though it is here. By doing so, we stand within God's story of radical hope. According to Isaiah, believing in God's future is believing in our future, as well. But it is even more than that. Believing in God's future is believing in everybody's future. In this way, we commit ourselves to the purpose of the world, under the loving power of God. We just need to put our hope into actions for it to be translated into a visible reality.

Czeslaw Milosz, survivor of a Nazi prison camp in Poland, became a very hopeful individual later in life, as he pressed on to live a free life in other countries and finally in America. During his time in America, he taught at Berkeley and was awarded the Nobel Prize for literature. It was in America that he wrote the celebrated poem "If There Is No God." In it, we hear some of his embedded empathy and love for people emerge in a

1. Milosz, *Poems*, 249.

whimsically fresh way. He writes, "If there is no God, / Not everything is permitted to man. / He is still his brother's keeper / And he is not permitted to sadden his brother, / By saying there is no God." In this brief poem, he awakens us to a radical hope and love for the person who doesn't believe in God and for those who do. His solidarity with others draws him to the conclusion that even if you do not believe in God, it is not OK to cause pain to someone who does believe in God by announcing to them, "There is no God." This shows a radical hope in the actions of radical respect.

As children we all learned the little song, "Sticks and stones may break my bones, but words can never hurt me." I am close to seventy now and have learned through the years that this is not true. Words are the things that hurt us the most. They last longer, hurt deeper, and leave lasting scars, more than the physical ones we carry. Therefore, we must be respectful with our words and how we say them. Words must carry a deep respect and care for the individual with whom we are talking. Hope cannot exist without this. Each step we take in fulfilling God's story must carry with it a respect that nurtures our neighbors. Milosz is right when he says we are not permitted to sadden the heart of those who believe in God, who believe in hope, by telling them that there belief is worthless. It lacks the kind of respect necessary to build communities of love.

During this time when our nerves are on edge, when the darkness of quarantine is getting to us and we just want to break out of our prison, let us be respectful. Remember that hope emerges through the silence of respect. A soft and gentle voice can turn anger and frustration into a peaceful rest. As my mother, and I suppose all our mothers, used to say, "If you don't have anything helpful to say, then don't say it." She was not very good, however, at her own advice. I, too, was not that great about taking it. But I do remember it. We cannot deepen humanity's hopeful experience if we keep forgetting what our mothers tried to teach us. That would be unforgiveable.

Struggling against Resignation

April 17, 2020

Mark 5:25–35 (NRSV)

Now there was a woman who had been suffering from hemorrhages for twelve years. She had endured much under many physicians, and had spent all that she had; and she was no better, but rather grew worse. She had heard about Jesus, and came up behind him in the crowd and touched his cloak, for she said, "If I but touch his clothes, I will be made well." Immediately her hemorrhage stopped; and she felt in her body that she was healed of her disease. Immediately aware that power had gone forth from him, Jesus turned about in the crowd and said, "Who touched my clothes?" And his disciples said to him, "You see the crowd pressing in on you; how can you say, 'Who touched me?'" He looked all around to see who had done it. But the woman, knowing what had happened to her, came in fear and trembling, fell down before him, and told him the whole truth. He said to her, "Daughter, your faith has made you well; go in peace, and be healed of your disease."

THE WOMAN IN THIS story can be described in two words: desperate and invisible. Mark tells us that she has spent all her money on doctors in hope of a cure and that she came out of the crowd as an invisible person to touch Jesus. She was hoping against hope that something might happen as she intersected Jesus's life. There is even more that Mark tells us about her invisibility. According to the sequence of events, this woman was an afterthought, an incidental encounter on the way to Jairus's daughter, who was very sick. While Jesus was on the way to Jairus's house, this woman came out of the crowd. She touched his coat, and she knew she was healed. Her feeling of desperation did not stop her from pressing on in the struggle against resigning herself to her misfortune and in her desire for a hopeful life of health, so she came out of the shadows.

In many stories like this, you might think that, once she was healed, the story was over. She could carry on with her life, go out in public, be with friends, and even go to synagogue. But it wasn't over for her or for Jesus. Twelve years of suffering needed a skilled healer to help her overcome her spiritual depletion. Jesus, that skilled and compassionate healer, found a way to help her towards a spiritual liberation, brought on by years of wondering where God was in her illness. After her healing, he instructed his disciples to find the person who touched him. A strange request, as the disciples acknowledged, seeing that so many people were around him and touched him. So, they went out demanding the one who touched Jesus to come forward. Of course, that could have been anyone. But this woman knew what they meant. She touched him unceremoniously, taking with her part of his power. Eventually, she came out from her invisibility and showed herself to Jesus in fear. She was forced to come out of the shadows, to face her actions and possible judgement.

But when she was brought to Jesus, she received neither judgment nor humiliation. She received words and touch, compassionate words to liberate her from her spiritual depletion. The words and actions were simple and somewhat strange. But they were healing. Jesus told her, "Daughter, your faith has made you well; go in peace, and be healed of your disease." Jesus didn't say it was God's power or even his power that healed her, but her faith. By using this phrase, he restored her depleted spiritual faith and let her know that even in her desperation, God was still present in her and in the world. Her struggle against resignation had brought her to the source of all healing: Jesus. In him, she found a way out of her desperation and prison of invisibility. We can find this as well, even when we are at our most desperate.

Our prisons are not necessarily the walls that surround us during the time of this visitation, of our invisible enemy. Our prisons are the confinement of spirit, in the resignation we bring to this isolation, not knowing that the key to our liberation is already in our hand: Faith.

Peace I Leave You

April 20, 2020

John 14:27 (NRSV)

Peace I leave with you; my peace I give to you. I do not give to you as the world gives. Do not let your hearts be troubled, and do not let them be afraid.

THERE IS A COMMON assumption, and not a completely accurate one, that peace is the absence of conflict, anxiety, fear, and turmoil. When we define peace through this conventional understanding, it focuses our attention on staying away from conflict and anxiety-producing situations—which leads us to conclude that peace can be achieved only in an antiseptic or a serene environment, in which hardly anything is asked of us. We have only to negotiate the silence and our inner thoughts, building in habits that keep us calm. But there is a problem with this; there are other people you cannot control. Furthermore, trying to escape from the world also prevents us from finding a purpose, sharpened through the experience of having to negotiate life's struggles.

In the end, peace is not the absence of pain and frustration. In fact, it is frustration and pain that drive us to seek a way to find the meaning of peace. Without the struggle, we can't find a way through the labyrinth of fear to find a true spiritual experience of peace. When Jesus sent the disciples into the world with the promise "Peace I leave with you; my peace I give to you," he did not send them into a world devoid of conflict. Just the opposite is true. He sent them into a world that mirrored his own, a world that would continue to fight against what God is asking of us and what Jesus is teaching. The disciples would be up against some of the most frightening experiences of their life. Some would lose their lives, as well. But, through all of it, they would carry the peace of Jesus. They would carry the purpose of Jesus into every part of the world. They would make authorities angry, they would bring good news to those that hear, and they would be tempted many times to put it all behind them, to live a more comfortable life. This is life, and it is difficult.

Of course, this does not mean that we shouldn't seek shelter from time to time. It is good to seek the solitude of the wind and trees, devoid of human contamination. But this is not the goal; it is a respite that can be experienced for only a time, before it becomes an escape and not a healing. Peace is not necessarily something we get from the silence; it is something we bring into the silence. Peace is more about faith and knowledge than it is about controlling our environment. Taking Jesus into the hard moments of life, knowing that no one can really destroy our peace, is where life and faith begin to merge together. Paul says it most clearly in Romans 8: "For I am convinced that neither death, nor life, nor angels, nor rulers, nor things present, nor things to come, nor powers, nor height, nor depth, nor anything else in all creation, will be able to separate us from the love of God in Christ Jesus our Lord" (Rom 8:36–38 NIV). It is in this knowledge that our peace is developed and nourished.

It behooves us when the world gets frustrating and chaotic to first dive in to what is happening, with the peace and love of God, enticing our heart to reach out. If you need to take a walk through the silence, then do it. But don't stay too long. Find your peace in walking through the fire, with Jesus holding you up. Then you will find the "peace that passes (goes beyond) all understanding." In the end, peace is what comes to us to affirm the love of God. It is a deep and abiding knowledge of God's desire to embrace us, as we struggle through the storm of life.

The Season of Fear

April 22, 2020

I John 4:18 (NRSV)

There is no fear in love, but perfect love casts out fear;
for fear has to do with punishment,
and whoever fears has not reached perfection in love.

"Nothing is harder to bear than a succession of fair days."

—*GOETHE*

I BELIEVE THERE IS little doubt that the world is under a cloud of fear, even though we pick up ourselves each day with hope and face the reality of this pandemic, this invisible enemy. We find it hard to live in the uncertainty of this invisible rain. Life is hard enough without having to negotiate living in an environment that is dangerous to all of us. Zygmunt Bauman writes, "Living under conditions of prolonged and apparently incurable uncertainty portends two similarly humiliating sensations: of ignorance (not knowing what the future will bring) and impotence (being unable to influence its course)."[1] His point is well taken. If we knew it would be only a month and all would be over, and we could get back to habits of normalcy, we would be less susceptible to fear. But not knowing and living so long under these conditions does take its toll on our spiritual vibrancy.

1. Bauman, *Moral Blindness*, 100.

But there is something we can do to diminish the fear that wants to overtake us: we can turn to love. While Bauman is right in his analysis of the hardship of living in the "impotence" of not being able to change our present situation, he has forgotten the spiritual dynamic of love that moves us to others, taking our eyes off ourselves. After all, thinking about only ourselves creates the very fear that we are trying to dissolve. Only love can exorcise the panic we experience in living under these conditions for a prolonged time. John, the disciple, is a much better architect of the spiritual life than Dr. Bauman on this point. He understands what we need in order to free ourselves from the desperate feelings of living in a pandemic. We need that unique experience of connecting with other human beings who suffer under the same uncertainty.

Think for a moment of the cloud that Jesus lived under for the three years of his ministry. His hardship was knowing how it would end and knowing when. His disciples, on the other hand, lived under the gift of Jesus's leadership, not knowing what was going to happen. Each perspective of life has its burden, but I would put the greater suffering on Jesus. Knowing what is about to come upon us, with certainty, is a burden none of us can really experience.

While many might say that fear is the master of this season, I believe that John is the real voice of this age: "There is no fear in love, but perfect love casts out fear" (1 John 4:18). The reason love has the power to cast out fear is because love grows out of the experience of community, and fear grows out of a sense of loneliness. When we are connected with others, we feel their emotions, we can live in their shoes, thereby providing us comfort in knowing we are not alone. Fear grows out of a sense of our isolation, leaving us the feeling that no one is there to help. In this season of fear, let us banish our isolation and reach out to each other in the hope of setting loose God's love inside us and giving it as a gift to those around us. This will make our days fairer and less difficult to suffer.

Emptiness with a Purpose

April 24, 2020

Ecclesiastes 4:1–4 (NRSV)

Again, I saw all the oppressions that are practiced under the sun. Look, the tears of the oppressed—with no one to comfort them! On the side of their oppressors there was power—with no one to comfort them. And I thought the dead, who have already died, more fortunate than the living, who are still alive; but better than both is the one who has not yet been, and has not seen the evil deeds that are done under the sun. Then I saw that all toil and all skill in work come from one person's envy of another. This also is vanity and a chasing after wind.

I HAVE FOUND OVER the years that Ecclesiastes has a profound message that is misunderstood. The above paragraph is an example of what I mean. In the first verse, the pain and empathy expressed by the Great Preacher over the mistreated in his kingdom, by those who care for nothing but themselves, gives him pause. He is moved by the injustice. But we tend to miss his point as we read the following three verses that suggest it is better never to have been born. We make a false conclusion if we think that he believes despair is the only proper response to the injustice of the world. Tears are also a proper response.

Let me ask you, have you ever been so sad at the state of affairs in the world that you have said, "I wish I was not here to see this." It is empathy that drives these statements. It turns to despair when you don't believe you can do anything about it—even if you are king. Ecclesiastes isn't about vanity, emptiness, or despair as the only solution. It is about empathy, compassion, and sympathy, which come from God. It is not a paradox. It is a confluence of emotional outpourings.

I love the works of Vincent van Gogh. His vision of beauty and use of bright colors expose the hope that fills his heart. But recently, I have taken to studying his early work, which are mainly sketches and dark oils of poor farmers. These early works came on the heels of his failed attempt at being a missionary to the peasants in Etten and Nuenen. It was also during this time that his father died, the father with whom he shared a stormy relationship. During this turbulent time, he took to drawing the peasants of the villages. None of them were happy pictures. Their faces were hard and drawn. But there is something about them that proclaims their heroic nature and, in return, brings out Vincent's empathy for their plight. My favorite lithograph and painting of this period is *The Potato Eaters*. The scene is of men, women, and children at a very simple table, with simple ragged Dutch clothing, having dinner. All they have on the table is tea and potatoes. There is hardly any light in the room, and the walls are dingy and unclean.

It is no secret that Vincent was in a state of despair at this time, but it didn't prevent him from reaching out with empathy, as if he were saying, "I am one of you." Eventually, his sadness overcame him. He had to be rescued by his brother Theo, who took care of him his whole life. Theo and Vincent died around the same time, one not being able to live without the other. Devotion and love filled their lives for each other, but it could never really heal Vincent's despair.

We might want to say like the Great Preacher of Ecclesiastes, "O that I had not been born, so I would not know of Vincent's life." But that is the sadness talking. Why not say, "O what a life that provided such light!" Through one of his paintings, whether it be *The Potato Eaters* or *The Starry Night*, there shines an instrument of God for the benefit of all who are in despair. He reached through his darkness to find the beauty that stood beyond his reach. This is compassion and empathy.

Joy Rediscovered

April 27, 2020

Psalm 126:4–6 (NEB)

O Lord, restore our well-being,

just as the streams in the arid south are replenished.

Those who shed tears as they plant

will shout for joy when they reap the harvest.

The one who weeps as he walks along, carrying his bag of seed,

will certainly come in with a shout of joy, carrying his sheaves of grain.

THE PSALMIST, WHO WROTE this above lament and praise, is remembering the suffering of Israel and most likely of himself. His experience of spiritual dryness has left him destitute and thirsty. The image used to describe this condition is the dry and empty land that has received little rain, little refreshment. It is the land of the Negeb, which is known for its desertlike conditions. When compared to our interior life, these images speak of a lifeless and joyless existence. The seeds that the farmer is scattering fill his mind with the hopeless possibility of them ever sprouting. The picture is one of a useless activity that has little hope of bringing forth any crop for good use. It is a sad picture of how life can sometimes be. But the refrain of this lament is certainly vibrant. The psalmist sees that one who sows the seeds in discontent will certainly arise someday, singing shouts of joy, when the rain comes to give needed refreshment to the crop. Soon there will be a harvest of grain that will turn the past suffering into an empty memory. How can you live in the remembered suffering of the past when you are "carrying sheaves of grain"?

It seems that the present world is carrying its bag of seeds, throwing them out on arid ground, hoping that the rain will bring life to these seeds of pain. But that is only part of the story. While we are all carrying our bags of seeds, the rain is in the near distance, ready to fall on our frustrated lives. While we are secured in our houses, we need only to lift our eyes and see the rain in the distance. God's refreshment, which will calm our frustration and sadness over our present crisis, is coming. But still we need to keep sowing our seeds, even if it seems hopeless. Joy will come, not through our own making, but as a surprise that could be just around the corner.

Eugene Peterson, translator of *The Message*, has said, "The psalm does not give us this joy as a package or as a formula, but there are some things it does do. It shows up the tininess of the world's joy and affirms the solidity of God's joy."[1] The one thing I do know about joy is this: it creates laughter. Joy makes us feel silly about our fretting and frustration of sowing our seeds in discontent. Laughter helps us say, "Was that really necessary, to be so despairing?" We should have had our eyes on the rain in the near distance. But we have a hard time raising up our eyes to see that far. It is hard to see the healing of God coming to save us. So, when it does come, our smile widens until it turns to laughter. It is then that we realize we were so silly and extremely tiny, to think that God could not bring the rain of joy into our life.

If we want this joy to come to us, the one thing we mustn't do is to try to engineer some spiritual shallowness that convinces us to always keep smiling, even when we are hurting so badly. We must sow our seeds in discontent before they can yield a crop of abundant joy. We must toil before we gather the fruits of our labor. Then, of course, we must wait for God to rain his healing on us, turning our grimace into a smile of laughter. Laughter doesn't come from a false spirituality; it comes from God, who awakens us.

1. Peterson, *Long Obedience*, 96.

Partnership with the Suffering of God

April 28, 2020

Romans 8:26–30 (NRSV)

Likewise the Spirit helps us in our weakness; for we do not know how to pray as we ought, but that very Spirit intercedes with sighs too deep for words. And God, who searches the heart, knows what is the mind of the Spirit, because the Spirit intercedes for the saints according to the will of God. We know that all things work together for good for those who love God, who are called according to his purpose.

SINCE WWII, THEOLOGIANS HAVE taken up the insight by Dietrich Bonhoeffer, "Only the suffering God can help."[1] Books on the pain of God, the vulnerability of God, and the heartbreak of God have helped pastors over these seventy years come to grips with the tragedy of those days. From these insights, we have gained a new understanding of God. But we must be clear. God does not suffer in the way we do. God does not suffer the pain of not knowing the future, the pain of death, or the worry and anxiety of our present circumstances. God suffers with us and even because of us. God's love for us is so strong that his longing to liberate us drove the Father to offer the Son on the cross. In this way, God's pain grew deeper and more profound. When Paul says in Romans 8:26, "Likewise the Spirit helps us in

---

1. Bonhoeffer, *Letters and Papers*, 332.

our weakness; for we do not know how to pray as we ought, but that very Spirit intercedes with sighs too deep for words," Paul is letting us into the very heart of God. When the Spirit, which is God, intercedes with sighs too deep for words, Paul is letting us into the secret: God suffers with us in order to help us grow deeper into our earthly life, which is now a world torn apart.

The Spirit helps us in two ways. First, when we step into our usual place to meet God, we find it frightening, yet joyful. We don't know what to say. We stammer words of incoherence. In this stammering communication, there is often pain or frustration. This is why Paul says that the Spirit is there in our stammerings. You are not alone. God in fact is suffering with you, helping you make clear what is in your heart. This is indeed a spiritual help. Throughout these stammerings, God helps us talk through our ignorance and pain.

Second, Paul reassures us that God searches our heart, and because the Spirit is a member of the Trinity, God knows how the Spirit arrives to help us. The combination of this communication before God then becomes clear to God. But the more helpful event that follows is this: we are touched by the experience that takes place in our conversation with God, through the work of the Spirit. This is indeed helpful. Even though we might enter prayer ignorant and empty, the Spirit awakens in us the very thoughts that bring our hearts closer to God. Therefore, the pain that causes us to stammer becomes a beautiful voice of joy and understanding.

Finally, Paul again reassures us with the words, "We know that all things work together for good for those who love God." Even within the limits of our understanding, Paul lets us know that God is going to work things out. Of course, this does not mean that he will heal everybody, or make everything we want come to pass. What he means is that God has a way of taking our suffering and turning it into a glimmer of hope. Why does God do this? Because he is the Suffering God, who suffers with us. God enlists those who suffer, both with God and for God, into servants of grace for the betterment of the world. But only if we understand the intentions of God, through the embrace of the Spirit. To be partners with God is to be willing to suffer with God.

Stay Strong during Hard Times

April 29, 2020

Philippians 3:14–15

So, let's keep focused on that goal, those of us who want everything God has for us. If any of you have something else in mind, something less than total commitment, God will clear your blurred vision—you'll see it yet! We're on the right track, let's stay on it.

WE ALL KNOW HOW hard it is to stay focused when there is so much turmoil, noise, dissenting voices, and internal conflicts. There is a feeling that overwhelms us. When that feeling comes, we want to shut-down our pursuits, arrangements for the future, and conversations with others. There were times in my early ministry when I wanted to quit, change directions; in other words, get out of the game. The flood of images came over me of what it would be like to take a position that didn't require so much responsibility, a position that didn't come with the constant grumbling and competition over small matters. Whenever these feelings poured through me, I thought of becoming a postal worker. I know it is a hard job, but it didn't seem to require my efforts in leading a group of people into ministry. But every time I did, I was brought back to my calling and to the voices that knew where I should be. At times, it was hard to take. I didn't want to do this anymore. Couldn't God and others see it was tearing me apart? But then I took time to rest, got up, and pursued my calling, each time with more understanding of how deficient I was at this work. But my reflections were necessary, in order to keep me committed to the goal God put before me.

In this letter to the Philippians, Paul was addressing a community of discouraged people when he wrote, "If any of you have something else in mind, something less than total commitment, God will clear your blurred vision—you'll see it yet! We're on the right track, let's stay on it" (Phil 4:14–15). Perhaps he was writing from his own experience of discouragement in the past, in order to make a connection with his community. Maybe his present frustration and fear of being in prison prompted his direct call to stay strong. He might have even been writing more to himself about staying strong than to others. It is often the case that we write about what we need to hear, in the process of writing to others. Whatever the case, his words formed a present connection with his hearers, who needed encouragement during some desperate time in the church. This tells you everything you need to know about Paul's focus. It was on them.

However we might say it, whatever words we might utter, the church universal is going through some desperate times in trying to find a connection with each other while being quarantined. The isolation is finally taking its toll on our capacity to feel a part of the world. For us who are suffering with physical ailments, we are having an even more difficult time because of our need for treatment; we are fighting hard to keep our heads up. We are also in need of encouragement. In times like this, we need the spiritual encouragement of God and the experience of the Spirit's peace of mind. These are necessary to keep us grounded in the reality in which we live, so that we don't constantly feel like jumping out of our skin. There is nothing more spiritually relaxing than knowing that our life still has a purpose, no matter how desperate we feel, no matter how isolated. We are called to remain committed by focusing on the goals set before us by the Prince of Peace. So, keep these words in your heart, under your hat, and right in front of you, "So, let's keep focused on that goal, those of us who want everything God has for us. If any of you have something else in mind, something less than total commitment, God will clear your blurred vision—you'll see it yet! We're on the right track, let's stay on it" (Phil 4:14–15).

Surprised by Love

May 1, 2020

Poor naked wretches, wheresoe'er you are,
That bide the pelting of the pitiless storm,
How shall your houseless heads and unfed sides,
Your loop'd and window'd raggedness,
Defend you from seasons such as these?

—Shakespeare, King Lear, Act III, Scene 4

A HIGH SCHOOL CLASS was reading *King Lear* and they were about to embark on Act III, Scene 4, where Lear and Edgar are in a tent outside Gloucester Castle, with a storm raging outside. Lear has gone completely mad, but he is trying to hang on to what sanity he has left. As the storm rages, Lear steps out of the tent and utters these immortal words, "Poor naked wretches . . . that bide the pelting of this pitiless storm." It was then that the teacher opened discussion in the classroom about the meaning of these words. The room was silent, until a young girl, a cheerleader for the football team, raised her hand and said, "I think he is praying." The rest of the class joined in a chorus of laughter, probably thinking what an airhead she was to think such a dumb thing. But then the teacher intervened, saying, "Tell me more about what you mean." The girl then described the transformation of Lear, moving from being mean to being kinder. She heard in Lear's words a kind of lament and prayer that she might have heard at church.

This short story was told by Frederick Buechner,[1] who was the teacher in the classroom. He ended this short story with a tribute to this young girl, who he believed saw something in this mad king. He said of her that it was probably her finest moment, when she changed and captured the minds of her fellow students. He hoped they would never look at her as just a cheerleader anymore, someone who didn't think about anyone but herself. The truth is that on that day, the others in the classroom were thinking only about themselves.

In this moment, this young girl and Lear were compatriots of compassion. They were both trying to find their identity, their selves, in the midst of people who had already labeled them. One was an airhead, the other was insane. But at one moment in history, several hundred years apart, they both showed the world their sensitive heart, their intelligent selves. They both understood that those that suffer the world's "slings and arrows" are to be pitied. And more than that, they, too, are to be pitied for being misunderstood for being compassionate. They both saw something in people that deserves our prayers. The world is indiscriminate when it comes to dishing out suffering on people. It is not easy for the world to exchange judgment for pity. It just means opening your heart to love and pain.

Each one of us has stories like this in our history, even as we are isolated from others, and watching the number of deaths climb as a result of this virus. Every number is a life, and every life has a story. We will never know all the stories of those who have been taken from us, but we have ours with which to compare them. What we want, feel, and long for in life is the same as those who have been taken from us. They wanted us to understand and comfort the pain in which they lived during the time of their illness. It makes me smile to think that a young high school girl opened up a new connection to *King Lear*. Shakespeare would be proud that he brought two such different people together, in one moment of history, to confront the world with their compassion.

---

1. Buechner, *Telling the Truth*, 26–31.

Shadows that Speak

May 4, 2020

DURING THIS SEASON OF isolation, I have taken to watching the birds outside the window where I sit, writing and reading. I have not taken the opportunity before to let my eyes wander to the activities of nature in such an attentive way. It moves, breathes, changes, and lives by an invisible mind, but with power. In these reflective times, it is important to watch and reflect on things we have overlooked because we move too fast. Poetry is one of the things I have neglected throughout the years, but now I see it as a language I know and enjoy. During these several weeks of isolation, God has directed my ears to the poets I have neglected. One whom I have particularly enjoyed throughout these recent times is Octavio Paz. He is a Mexican poet, Nobel Laureate, and a man who sees what most of us do not. He is in touch with nature and knows some of its secrets and its power to illuminate. He also sees in nature the very transitory essence of all living things. It does not make him sad, but instead, he sees within this fleshly life a wonderful beauty that cannot be replaced. One of the passages in his celebrated poem "A Draft of Shadows" goes like this:

> Noon:
> the trees in the patio are green flames.
> The crackling of the last embers
> in the grass: stubborn insects.
> Over the yellow meadows,
> clarities: the glass footsteps of autumn.
> A fortuitous meeting of reflections,
> an ephemeral bird

enters the foliage of these letters.
The sun, in my writing, drinks the shadows.
Between the walls—not of stone,
but raised by memory—
a transitory grove:
Reflective light among the trunks
and the breathing of the wind.[1]

Peter and Paul, those dutiful disciples, both understood that the world is transitory (flesh), but mainly within the context of proclaiming that God's Word lasts forever. But I would like to think they also understood nature the way Octavio Paz did. They must have seen the hand of God moving the trees, the breath of God creating the wind, and the heart of God creating beauty. We must not forget that nature speaks. The shadows of the trees, birds, and flowers speak as well. Nature moves as God walks through the garden, providing color and the possibility of endless words to describe the beauty we see, which God created.

So, when you walk past your windows this week, take time to look outside to watch the shadows of nature and the visible presence of God walking through your garden. As God passes through the flowers, disturbs the trees, and leaves the footprints of an endearing heart on the grass where God walked, press your lips to sing praises. You might even see Octavio Paz walking beside God trimming the flowers, in the midst of the shadows of the trees, working together to make a beautiful world.

1. Paz, *Poems*, 459.

In the End: Be Silent

May 6, 2020

Job 42:1–6

THE LAST WORDS THAT Job spoke to God are these:

> I'm convinced: You can do anything and everything.
>> Nothing and no one can upset your plans.
> You asked, "Who is this muddying the water,
>> ignorantly confusing the issue, second-guessing my purposes?"
> I admit it. I was the one. I babbled on about things far beyond me,
>> made small talk about wonders way over my head.
> You told me, "Listen, and let me do the talking.
>> Let me ask the questions. You give the answers."
> I admit I once lived by rumors of you;
>> now I have it all firsthand—from my own eyes and ears!
> I'm sorry—forgive me. I'll never do that again, I promise!
>> I'll never again live on crusts of hearsay, crumbs of rumor.

Most of us cannot help asking the question "why" when we are facing evil or suffering. It is as natural for us as caring for our children. But at the same time, we rarely get back an answer that satisfies. That is why Job is so instructive for the questioners of this world, who question God's action or inaction in the face of evil. Humility and silence are often the right move in these circumstances. We can still believe in God's goodness, without understanding everything about God. Throughout Job's ordeal, which we would agree was more than most could take, Job continued to plead his case and accuse God of injustice. He pleaded that he was righteous and therefore should not have been treated in such a despicable way. He demanded answers. His friends, on the other hand, had answers that were wrongheaded and mean. They believed that suffering comes from sin. From this simplistic view of life, they sprang into action against Job, demanding his repentance. This, they believed, was his only possibility of escaping his plague. Job stood against this rationale.

Through all his suffering, Job continued to press God for answers, but God pressed back with "I am God; who are you?" This constant response from God might seem cruel. But, in the end, it is instructive. Job's friends are the cruel ones. Their simplistic answer to the problem of evil lacks experience and sees God as a mechanistic monster. They believed God dishes out what people deserve. Therefore, if you suffer, if you lose your wealth, if unfortunate things happen to you or your children, it is because you have sinned and need to repent. I would suggest that this perspective lacks depth and has the potential of bringing evil into the world, more evil than those who suffer in silence before God. It is cruel and mean to suggest that those who contract a disease are more sinful than those who do not. This is not reflective of God's heart, nor is it helpful to humanity to carry this simplistic perspective into the world.

In this world of our invisible raider, I believe it is more helpful and true to admit, as Job did, that we often "babble on about things far beyond us." It is better to turn to God with arms open to receive his grace. That is what can be understood. We are far too limited to understand everything God is doing and why. Like Job we should confess, "I'm sorry—forgive me. I'll never do that again, I promise! I'll never again live on crusts of hearsay, crumbs of rumor." Wise words for all of us who suffer in this world. Learn to be silent before we start babbling about things about which we know nothing. Silence is a great teacher, not only of our interior life, but of the heart of God. In silence, we stand with the voices that have been our guide for years. It is when we babble that we are alone, hearing only one voice, our own.

Faith Has Reasons

May 15, 2020

Fides quaerens intellectum.

(I believe in order to understand.)

—St. Anselm

Most religions are based on a faith that recognizes the divide between what we can see and what we can't, what we can rationally prove and what we can't. Christianity is empowered by faith, which causes us to stretch our minds to grasp what we sometimes cannot understand. But there is a unique dynamic between faith and reason that we often overlook. Faith has reasons to believe in the life, purpose, and words of Jesus, which empowers us to take further steps to follow his direction. Faith is not a leap without confirmation. We follow Jesus because we are compelled by what we read and understand about who he is. That little bit of belief ushers us forward, which in turn convinces us further that Jesus is to be believed, by the experience of walking with him.

Every one of us has trusted friends. They have become our trusted friends because we have witnessed their character. We are recipients of their friendship and trust them as they live their lives. When we say "I believe in them," it is because of our relationship with them, and we know that we can count on them. The more we experience this trusted relationship, the more we are willing to risk our deepest secrets with them. Faith and belief in God or a friend are the first steps to understanding that person. We do not understand God from afar, but from taking our trust and growing it deeper into a relationship of love. Paul makes it clear that we are justified (brought closer into God's kingdom) by faith empowered through the Spirit, not by holding on to doctrines that define religious behavior. Understanding God's purpose is not discovered through this latter way; it flourishes as we are able to see more clearly through the Spirit's vision.

So, what does all this mean for us? What does it mean in times of difficulty, like now? It is no surprise that when difficulties enter our life, suffering is all we can see. It is hard to see beyond the trouble before us. But that is what faith is. Faith is a gift, established through our relationship with Jesus, that opens our eyes to understanding God's grace and love, beyond the pain that is bombarding us. Developing trust in God is essential for living a Christian life. The deeper we go, the less we see the darkness that is trying to blind us to God's goodness. We may not understand the reasons for all that is happening to us, but we can see God in the midst of our trouble. At times, we can actually hear God as well. God is saying, "Don't stop believing in me. Hang in there. We can get through this together."

When I think of how God helps us, I imagine the relationship of Jesus and his disciples. The disciples tend to be in constant turmoil. They worry, they fear, and they try to control the future through the mechanisms they learned in the past. Whenever Jesus senses that they are not progressing in faith, he does something radical. He sends them out to villages by themselves to heal and preach what they know. In other words, he creates more anxiety for them, which demands that they lean on God to stay centered. Faith is leaning on God, when God pushes us into the world for purposes beyond our understanding. But by Saint Anselm's example, "Believe in order to understand." Believe in the goodness of God, believe in the grace of God, and believe that God knows what He is doing. By believing you will learn how to lean on God and how-to live-in times of fear and anxiety.

Spiritual Maturity

May 18, 2020

Philippians 2:1–5

THERE ARE MANY DEFINITIONS for the word or the activity called spirituality. Some align it with charismatic features of having dreams or having spiritual gifts of healing. Some align it with mystical traditions of the eleventh through the fourteenth centuries, in which monks sought solitary avenues of life, creating traditions of silence, meditation, and prayer. Others, who are more cerebral in nature, have aligned this word with the study of Scripture, seeking patterns of discipline that arise out of the teaching and behavior of Jesus and Paul. Most likely, there are more nuances attached to this activity, which have given rise to many books and many experiments throughout history. The truth is that all these avenues of discovery have their place in the church. But what I see in all these endeavors is the desire to "grow up" or "to become mature." Each one of these traditions is trying to help the seeker of God's truth grow up in the image and character of Jesus. Each path has its own hardships, and each has its own understanding of what spiritual maturity really means.

Paul speaks of spirituality in terms of how we live with others in the church and our community. While he was a deeply spiritual man, having an inward life that sought the closeness of Jesus, he was, in the end, a very practical man. He reminds me of Dietrich Bonhoeffer, who was also a deeply spiritual man and also someone who saw that spirituality, in the end, is about making tough decisions and growing up to live in the maturity of Christ. Spiritual maturity is seeing the world for what it and what it can become. Therefore, it is about becoming a mature person in a world of those who just want the trappings of power and prestige but refuse to act in a mature way. Paul's letter to the Philippians opens up a dialogue with those in the church who are working on growing up in Christ. Paul makes his most poignant statement in Philippians 2: 1–5:

> If then there is any encouragement in Christ, any consolation from love, any sharing in the Spirit, any compassion and sympathy, make my joy complete: be of the same mind, having the same love, being in full accord and of one mind. Do nothing from selfish ambition or conceit, but in humility regard others as better than yourselves. Let each of you look not to your own interests, but to the interests of others. Let the same mind be in you that was in Christ Jesus. (NRSV)

The last sentence of this beautiful passage stands out for me: "Let the same mind be in you that was in Christ Jesus." This is the quintessential goal of the mature Christian living. We can all talk about being humble, thinking of others, and eradicating our selfishness, but it all comes down to this: develop the same mind, attitude, and direction as Jesus, who was the greatest demonstration of human maturity in history! Maturity, simply put, is growing up. It is developing a poise in life that cannot be shaken, only bent. For having poise is showing our ability to bend with adversity, developing flexibility within a strong vision for the future, without cracking. If we cannot bend with poise, we will crack, exposing the hard shell we have built around us, through resistance. So, like Jesus, let your inner flexibility be exposed constantly. It will prevent the pain of breaking, as the adversity of life tries to cut you down. Maturity is God's answer to false religiosity, that cracks when suffering becomes a reality, instead of something we try to forget.

Breaking the Cycle

May 23, 2020

Matthew 6:33-34 (NIV)

But strive first for the kingdom of God and his righteousness,

and all these things will be given to you as well.

So do not worry about tomorrow,

for tomorrow will bring worries of its own.

Today's trouble is enough for today.

IT IS PART OF the working mind that when someone says don't think about something, that is all we do. We think about it obsessively, like a dog chasing its tail. We continue to let it wind around our mind until we are exhausted. This is especially true when that something about which we are not supposed to think is the object of our anxiety and fear. When I was in elementary school, one of my teachers used to play a game with all of us. He would say, "Don't think about an apple!" Then he would ask us, "Did you think about an apple?" Of course, we all said yes. I think it was his way of teaching us the power of persuasion. We are influenced by suggestion, even though we don't even know it.

When Jesus says "Don't worry about tomorrow, tomorrow will have enough trouble of its own," all we do is think about money, kids, sickness, and other things that trigger our anxiety. So, there is a certain amount of hilarity in Jesus' statement, because he stimulates the very thing in us that he is trying to defuse. I don't believe he is talking about being overwhelmed with our occupations, the jobs that often consume us, but about our preoccupations, the things we worry about, long before anything happens. To be preoccupied is to be enslaved to the spinning of the mind over things that haven't yet arrived in our life, so we try to control our tiny world to divert their effects.

I have been told that I am not very fun on road trips with the family. I am obsessed about planning everything to the minute. When we get too far off schedule, I start to get the jitters. I worry that we are going to miss something I planned, or we are going to miss an appointment I made to go through a museum or historical site. For the most part, it always turns out. But I worry and fret about the most minor things. When that happens, fun goes out the window. Relaxation flies away and rarely returns. In other words, life doesn't carry with it the joy it had before we left on the trip. This is why I like cruises. You get on the ship, and someone else takes you to places without the worry of trying to get there. I also enjoy that during the time on the ship, there is a spa and a bar to help me relax with my wife, as we think about what to eat.

I believe we are all exhausted from this experience of self-quarantine, not necessarily by the isolation or the frustration of not being able to go to our favorite restaurant, or to visit and mingle among the people we care about, but because we are preoccupied with the virus itself. When is it going to retreat? Who will it affect next? Will someone I love be infected? The constant preoccupation with its presence in our world can't help but stimulate our fear and worry. But it is Jesus's desire that all this worry retreat from our minds. It only brings further loss of joy, the joy that we were designed to experience. So, turn off the television coverage of the virus and don't think about it. Gotcha. You didn't think about it, right?

Let your mind wander off into the life of Jesus, imagining him talking with the people he loves and whom he desires to have joy. Imagine his smile, his easiness, his hands, his face. Think on these things, and let the joy fly back into your life.

The Power of Music

May 25, 2020

1 Samuel 16:23 (NIV)

And whenever the evil spirit from God came upon Saul,

David took the lyre and played it with his hand,

and Saul would be relieved and feel better,

and the evil spirit would depart from him.

IT IS SAID THAT Saul used to summon David in to play music for him, in order to calm his troubled spirit. I Samuel 16:23 recounts one of these times. Saul was under constant pressure from his insecurities and fears, regarding what others felt about him and what they were conspiring to do against him. These thoughts made him an erratic leader and an unstable captain of his army. Music provided some relief to these troubling thoughts that drove him to the point of madness. Music has always had this calming and soothing effect on the human heart. There is something to which we connect in its beat, its melody, and its hopeful longing. Music can also move our feet to dance and our hearts to sing, which provides a feeling of excitement and energy. Like poetry, music has a rhythm that plays us, as we try to enter the sounds and words that are designed to transport us.

I have recently downloaded the new album by Andrea Bocelli entitled *Sì*. Even though there are instruments that play in the background, his voice is a full and complete instrument in itself. It carries you to the core of that string inside you, that, when plucked, soothes all the tension and worry you have been carrying around. During the day, I am in need of such a striking of that chord that can liberate me from my own concerns and my weariness as well. That smooth and finely tuned voice is able to make words come alive in me. But at other times during the day, I like to listen to Jimi Hendrix. His driving guitar opens up that part of me that wants to crash through my walls and grab something real in which to carry me throughout the day. His guitar is powerful, and when we allow it to carry us into ourselves, we can feel just a little bit of that power to create things in the world. I have been treating myself especially to "All Along the Watchtower" and "Little Wing." They show off his talent to make the guitar sing.

Both Bocelli and Hendrix connect with something deep in us. Bocelli is like Mozart, who allows the violins to hang over the melody like a rainbow of color. Hendrix is like Beethoven, who wishes to conquer something, instead of allowing the music to sooth you. Beethoven wants you to feel the music through its power; Mozart wants you to feel the music through its subtle tones and melodies.

Music is spiritual. Every religion creates its music to help the worshipper develop the spirituality behind the story of its god. Christians have developed music throughout the centuries to tell the story of Jesus, but also to help the worshipper feel the spirituality behind the story. Like Beethoven, Jesus was powerful and driven. His spiritual message was hard. But Jesus was also gracious and loving. As in the story of the woman who poured perfume on Jesus's feet, you can hear the violins softly entering the melody of the story, which offers us the tears and sighs of a loving spiritual presence.

During this time of our invisible enemy, don't forget to listen to music. But the most important thing we can do is to let it play us. Let it pluck that chord that unlocks the spiritual treasure with which we were born. Especially during this time, we need to make a habit of putting down everything we are doing and just listening to something that drains our anxieties and heightens our joy of being played by music.

Hiding the Gospel in Ourselves

June 1, 2020

Psalm 2:1–3

Why the big noise, nations?

Why the mean plots, peoples?

Earth-leaders push for position,

Demagogues and delegates meet for summit talks,

The God-deniers, the Messiah-defiers:

"Let's get free of God!

Cast loose from Messiah!"

Heaven-throned God breaks out laughing.

ALMOST TWO HUNDRED YEARS ago, a French historian came to America to discover what makes America tick. He desired to unlock its character, which had led to a strong democracy. His name was Alexis de Tocqueville. His two-volume work has stood the test of time, providing American historians continued insights regarding the founding of our nation, its continual struggles with its original demons, and strong purpose. One of those demons is our fascination with individualistic goals, forgetting about our community responsibilities. In his second volume, Tocqueville writes of Americans, "Each citizen is habitually engaged in the contemplation of a very puny object, namely himself [herself]."[1] While we have, from time to time, broken free of this demon, showing great commitment to a larger cause, we still travel back to the comfort of this old friend. Last week I wrote a meditation entitled "Responsibility in an Age of Individualism." I would like to revisit its points in this meditation, in light of the recent acts of protest and violence, stemming from the killing of Mr. Floyd.

It is clear to me that systemic racism was present in the exercise of force in the killing of Mr. Floyd. It was not just one act of an angry white man. It is a systemic problem, which was evident in the other men at the scene and maybe even up the food chain. There are many reasons that racism tends to divide our nation more than other nations. But one reason is the one that Alexis de Tocqueville observed: our insatiable individualism and obsession with our own needs. These obsessions limit our freedom, especially in regard to a group of people with different behaviors. We become justified and emboldened to carry out acts against others, because we feel their intrusion. This is racism, clothed in justified anger, proclaiming our own human decency before a like-minded world.

When the psalmist cries out "Why the big noise, nations? Why the mean plots, peoples?," he is not asking a hypothetical question; he knows the answer. He knows that all nations are just big noise at times. They spin their nationalism against a hopeful stream of cooperation that could lead to peace and understanding. But instead, our own fascination with our glory gets in the way of recognizing anything outside ourselves. I love how he ends this first passage: "Heaven-throned God breaks out laughing." What a delightful sight. Can't you see it? God sitting in the heavens and bursting out with belly laughs at our stupidity. That is enough to make me want to reflect upon my own stupid racist thoughts. God laughing at you must be taken seriously. It is something that humbles us.

I hope that when we are sitting in our homes and watching the news that our shouts of disgust don't move to blaming others first. Our shouts should be of disgust with ourselves. We need to ask ourselves, "Is my self-interest getting in the way of seeing the way things are, and what it is that I should do?" We are in dangerous times that must be faced with as much understanding as possible. Finally, we need to pray. Pray for a leader who has the skill, poise, vision, and kindness to speak a message of clarity to both sides. Someone out of the crowd. Someone who doesn't hide the gospel inside himself or herself, but has the capacity to see how it works within a divided world.

1. Tocqueville, *Democracy*, 2:98–99.

Time for Peace

June 3, 2020

Ecclesiastes 3:7–8 (NIV)

a time to tear and a time to mend,
　　a time to be silent and a time to speak,
a time to love and a time to hate,
　　a time for war and a time for peace.

I HAVE RECENTLY WRITTEN about the unrest in our streets and in the hearts of Americans. This unrest is not absent from my heart either. I feel connected to all those feelings on the streets of our cities. I feel the anger of unrequited justice in the African American community, I feel the sadness of those connected with communities of poverty, and, in a strange way, I feel a connection with those that are exploiting this opportunity to steal from their brothers and sisters. But while I feel these things, I also have a hard time understanding many of them. These are the mysteries that keep me up at night, while I'm hoping that I will find some key to unlock my understanding of the hearts and minds of those on the streets that decide to bring harm to their communities instead of resolution.

Riots and protests are unpredictable events that can turn on one shout or one bottle thrown at another person. They are tense and rarely helpful. Most of us are looking for resolution to the problems being spoken about, which demands a steady understanding of the goals to be accomplished. But for me, at this moment, I wish for peace—peace of mind. Ecclesiastes is clearheaded about these matters, beginning with the understanding that everything has its time. The Preacher's goal is to help us rest in the knowledge that certain things have their time and then will be done. At this time, there is "tearing" and "war." But I am looking for a time of peace and silence. Not to run away, but to stand back in solitude to be able to draw a clearer picture of all that is happening. Like all of us, I need a time to heal.

Healing takes on so many different personalities. For some, healing is a surge of power that flows through the body, providing a sense of confidence and wellness. For others, it is the help that comes in the middle of a tragedy, allowing the fear of powerlessness to subside within the embrace of another. For me, healing comes from solitude, which settles my heart within the silence. It is not emptiness. Solitude is never empty, but filled with the soothing words of God that fill my space with a hopeful dream of tomorrow. But in order to find this space I must, like all of us, stop. I must stop the endless tasks that fill my day, the constant flow of responsibility that compels me to expend my energy for the good. I must also stop the endless flow of images from my television providing me with a flood of emotions that I cannot understand—and those I do turn me to angry thoughts. But even though I cannot understand in totality what moves many ugly events, I feel compelled to do something. But I don't know what that is. All I know is I must find that space that exists in the solitude of God's Word.

The question of how to help in a time of tearing down can be answered only in solitude. We must stop, in order to move forward. We must find love to avoid hate, and we must pray to find the answer to "What can I do in this sad time?" Unfortunately, COVID-19 does not provide us the means to stop. We are still busy. We all think and worry. Being at home, quarantined with a computer, is not the same as solitude. Solitude is stepping intentionally into a space filled with God's Word and love. It takes the pushing away of noise, which confuses the clarity of God's voice. God's voice is never noisy. Instead, it is a reassuring voice that calms my nerves, preventing me from making any angry gesture towards the unsurety of this present time.

Little Children

June 5, 2020

Luke 18:16 (NRSV)

But Jesus called for them and said,
"Let the little children come to me, and do not stop them;
for it is to such as these that the kingdom of God belongs.

I HAVE BEEN THINKING about little children lately, as I prepare to be a grandfather again, blessed with three already. I am amazed at their dependence on adults to get what they need to survive emotionally and physically. But I am even more amazed at their independence. As I watch my two-and-a-half-year-old granddaughter on FaceTime or Zoom, I realize that her days of complete dependence are over. Mom and Dad are there, but her world is suddenly growing past them. She wants to know that they are there, but only as an object of support. She is on the move to somewhere, but with no clear understanding where that is. She looks around for Mom and Dad, but just to know they are there. Once she sees them, she is off again to explore this mysterious world that is ready for her to take charge.

I don't know how old the children were that surrounded Jesus that day, but I bet you they were about two or three years old, like my granddaughter. They probably looked at their mom and dad to see if they were there, then ran off to embrace Jesus and explore this mysterious world. When they started to surround Jesus, the disciples became a little annoyed. They wanted Jesus to give his address to the crowed of adults, providing the good news that the world was changing and their lives could change with it. The disciples had an agenda, to which they expected Jesus to conform. The children were a distraction to the ultimate goal. But they missed the beauty of the moment, because they were too busy organizing the event for Jesus. But Jesus didn't. For the disciples, these children were messing up their plans. That is what children do. They force adults to rearrange their priorities. They get in the way of "the best laid schemes of mice and men." But that is their gift to the world.

When Jesus barked "Let the little children come to me, and do not stop them, for it is to such as these that the kingdom of God belongs," he recognized that what was planned would have to take a back seat. These children's world needed to expand. They needed to know that the man speaking about God was gentle, kind, and patient. They didn't need to go away from there, knowing that God has no time for them. Who knows what was going on in the lives of those young children? Some may have lost their mother, others their sibling, and some may even not have had enough to eat. But when they came to Jesus, the man who spoke of God, they knew that God had time for them and would hold their trouble in his heart.

How hard it must have been for them to hear that the man who spoke of God was executed on a cross. I am sure they thought, "How can a gentle man be killed just for being kind?" It was then that they needed someone patient to hear their pain, so they could go out and explore the mysteries of the world again.

In this time of isolation, let the little children come to us. Let our plans be changed for the sake of others. Let our children and our friends know, we have time for them. Offer them the most precious gift you have—yourself. Remember, with children, plans are meant to be changed. The same goes for adults. We need a little distraction now and then. We need to turn, make sure the world and family are still there, then explore a little part of the mysteries of the world.

Tell It Slant

June 8, 2020

Ephesians 4:15 (NIV)

But speaking the truth in love,
we must grow up in every way into him who is the head, into Christ.

Tell all the truth but tell it slant—
Success in Circuit lies
Too bright for our infirm Delight
The Truth's superb surprise
As Lightning to the Children eased
With explanation kind
The Truth must dazzle gradually
Or every man be blind—

—EMILY DICKINSON[1]

T.S. ELIOT, THAT CELEBRATED poet of "The Hollow Men" and "The Waste Land," created the following words in his poem "Burnt Norton": "[H]uman kind / Cannot bear very much reality."[2] When he wrote this,

---

1. Dickinson, *Complete Poems*, 506–507.
2. Eliot, *Complete Poems and Plays*, 118.

Eliot was already deeply embedded in his Catholicism, which provided him another point of view. When asked about the meaning of this text, he said that God must parcel out the truth in small doses, or we would be overwhelmed with the burdens of God's demands and our life, so much so, that we would be unable to function. Emily Dickinson, in her own way, says the same thing in her poem above: "Tell all the truth but tell it slant— / Success in Circuit lies / Too bright for our infirm Delight / The Truth's superb surprise."

What both Eliot and Dickinson know is that human beings are fragile. Their egos are subject to humiliation, their emotions submissive to suggestion, and their hearts open to temptation. Therefore, in order to communicate to others or to try to persuade others of our truth, we must "speak the truth in love," which proves that we are grown up and able to be trusted. We need to demonstrate that we are mature enough to speak within this fragileness, but speaking the truth as best we can. In a time like ours, when all we want to do is shout, we need to stand back and formulate words of truth that carry with them the feeling and warmth of love. I know that the time of shouting is not over, and whatever pain is in our communities will continue to be displayed through loud voices. That makes this a very dangerous time. Shouting does not communicate messages for solutions. It just creates chaotic noise.

There will be time for a more poised meeting in the future. When that happens, I hope there will not have been too much damage done. Those whose bruises and wounds go deep may not be able to enter into this next phase of negotiations with the clarity needed to protect their achieved goals or desired protections for others. I am hopeful that the world is ready to listen to grievances of the past and dreams for the future. But it will take everyone's effort in listening to Ms. Dickinson and Mr. Eliot, in order to work towards useful solutions. I love what Ms. Dickinson said in her last lines: "The Truth must dazzle gradually / Or every man be blind—." Wise words for all of us, for every time in our life. The truth must inspire, not destroy; it must overcome prejudices, cleansing the heart.

Yet, there is still one essential quest that must play a part in this path to truth-telling. We have to come to grips with the useful understanding that we are fragile, the speaker and the spoken-to. Observing the voice of God in Scripture is a useful tool for designing our words for this task. "Tell all the truth but tell it slant— / Success in Circuit lies." This is how God talks to us and how we are expected to talk with others.

Let Us Go to the House of the Lord

June 10, 2020

Psalm 122:1–2, 6–9 (NRSV)

I was glad when they said to me,
"Let us go to the house of the Lord!"
Our feet are standing
within your gates, O Jerusalem....
Pray for the peace of Jerusalem:
"May they prosper who love you.
Peace be within your walls,
and security within your towers."
For the sake of my relatives and friends
I will say, "Peace be within you."
For the sake of the house of the Lord our God,
I will seek your good.

"WORSHIP GIVES US A workable structure for life," says Eugene Peterson.[1] This is absolutely true. Worship is the thread that is woven through every

---

1. Peterson, *Long Obedience*, 47.

aspect of our spiritual existence. But before we begin to untangle the profound meaning of that phrase, we first need to take a stab at what it means to worship.

We often associate worship with going to a sanctuary, a meeting place, singing, listening to prayers, and listening to a sermon. These are all activities, I would suggest, that are inspired by worship and also increase our desire to worship. But while they form part of the patchwork quilt that is worship, they are not in themselves what the psalmist calls worship. When the psalmist says "Let us go to the house of the Lord," he means going to the temple. He desires to stand in the magnificent space, silent and holy. He desires to place himself before God with awe and reverence, without words, only the promptings of the Spirit that empower him to give his whole self to the infinite, holy God. Worship often happens without words, which then move us to do what is right and just in the world. The psalmist's last sentence is helpful in our endeavor to understand the act and effects of worship. He says, "For the sake of the house of the Lord our God, I will seek your good." Worship, in the psalmist's heart, is to create righteous and loving works that come from God. But they can only come from a still heart, captured in the moments we stand before God in the sacred places we have chosen or God has chosen.

In a world disjointed by unrest in our communities, worship is necessary to restore the peace within us. The purpose of worship is to honor God, and from this, God provides us peace within our conflicted hearts. It is hard to do what is right and just when we are filled with the anger of years of frustration and seeming political indifference. Those that march in the streets should pray "peace be with you all," before they hold their signs up before a watching world. It is the only way to make it an act of peace. We all must worship to connect with the holy God, who meets us and the people in the streets, in silence.

We don't need a sanctuary to worship, even though it is useful; we need a place inside us. We need only to prepare ourselves to walk into the peaceful solitude with God. This could be anywhere. It could be in a gathering, it could be in a room, it could be outside. It may seem strange to say, but you don't even need a preacher. You just need to be bathed in the Spirit of God who transforms us with the Word of God, turning our unrest into restful peace. When Eugene Peterson says "Worship gives us a workable structure for life," this is what he means. Worship inspires good works and the means to think through what those good works might look like, in a life that wants to follow God into the conflicted places of life. This workable structure for life is, in the end, nothing but the movements of mind and body, following the footsteps of Jesus.

And There Will Be Time . . .

June 15, 2020

And indeed there will be time
To wonder, "Do I dare?" and, "Do I dare?"
Time to turn back and descend the stair,
With a bald spot in the middle of my hair—

—T.S. ELIOT, "THE LOVE SONG OF J. ALFRED PRUFROCK"[1]

I HAVE ALWAYS ADMIRED T.S. Eliot's poem of 1915. He was immersed in a world war, as well as a cultural struggle to maintain the traditions of his adopted country of Britain. He was part of that movement in America and Britain that tried to articulate the malaise of the dying cultural characteristics of a Victorian society and its movement towards modernization. His early works characterized this dying culture as a "yellow fog" that was heavy but had no texture. His purpose was to try to lift this fog, to shed light upon the lives of people who were still trying to live within the goals of this dying culture.

His words and mood express the same as those of the great preacher of Ecclesiastes. Both set the mood by phrases that are depressing, but must be embraced to move past the passivity of which they speak. The great preacher says, "There is a time for war and a time for peace." Eliot says, "And indeed there will be time / To wonder, 'Do I dare?' and, 'Do I dare?'" These poets are not telling us to stop and give up. They are telling us to embrace the time; it is the only way to lift the "yellow fog." God created

---

1. Eliot, *Complete Poems and Plays*, 4.

days so that we could embrace the time in that day, to let it be ours to fill up with activity. God himself filled up each day with divine activity, creating a world for us. It is up to us to fill up the day to create a new kind of world for others. When we create this new future, the "yellow fog" lifts just a little. Its heaviness and formless body will blow away, so that we can see the light that is peeking in from around the corner to enjoy.

When time slips away from us, or if we feel it does, we are struck with an uncomfortable awareness of loss. We lost something. We lost a day, a week, a month, or even a life. That is a most depressing moment, when your reflections lead you to the conclusion that fear has stolen your life—especially when you thought all this time that fear would protect you. But, in the end, it actually stole the very thing you were trying to protect: life. Jesus's parables and his confrontations are all meant to move people in a forward direction to God. But it meant that people had to embrace the possibility of falling down the stairs to get out of the house. If we stand too long contemplating whether to descend the stairs, the easiest thing to do is to go back into our bedrooms and lie down.

During this time of "staying in," it does not mean we need to live in fear. "Staying in" means living in courage. It is courageous to make sure you save a life or keep it safe. You are doing something for someone else. You are living out the fulfilment of God's law, "Love your neighbor as yourself." That is the most courageous thing you can do. Then when it is time to go out, go out for others. Lift the "yellow fog" from around you, so that the many who have learned fear at this time, instead of courage, can be set free. If we don't, we will all live within the immortal words of J. Alfred Prufrock, "And indeed there will be time / To wonder, 'Do I dare?' and, 'Do I dare?' / Time to turn back and descend the stair, / With a bald spot in the middle of my hair."

Lamenting into Joy

June 17, 2020

Psalm 102:1–2, 12–14

God, listen! Listen to my prayer,
listen to the pain in my cries.
Don't turn your back on me
just when I need you so desperately.
Pay attention! This is a cry for help!
And hurry—this can't wait! . . .
Yet you, God, are sovereign still,
always and ever sovereign.
You'll get up from your throne and help Zion—
it's time for compassionate help.
Oh, how your servants love this city's rubble
and weep with compassion over its dust!

THE PSALMS WERE DESIGNED to be sung, but just not for making a joyful noise. They were first written to be prayed, to offer the worshipper a chance to enter God's holy place of pain. They were written to help us find our voice before a holy and compassionate God. To achieve this spiritual connection the choir directors of Israel created psalms of joy, psalms of praise, and psalms of lament. Walter Brueggemann, Old Testament professor, divides the psalms into psalms of orientation, disorientation, and new orientation. Each one of these kinds of psalms has its own purpose and use of language, giving it a special spiritual flavor.[1] Psalm 102 is a psalm of lament (disorientation). It is written to help the worshipper, who is lost and distressed, find peace through a series of words and images that connect with the pain of Israel and God's pain, as well. But the worshipper must dive in to the whole direction of the psalm before any healing can emerge. Words must be attached to emotions; honesty must become courageous before this lament can help us find some joy in life.

Many years ago, I was talking with a psychologist friend of mine, who had lost his son to a possible suicide. I had just lost my father to cancer. I was struggling with a kind of haunting despair. My father and I had many disagreements over our life together, mainly on the direction of my life. He thought that I was wasting my time becoming a pastor, with which I, too, struggled myself. When he died, we still had unresolved issues between us and memories of frustrating conversations. I told all this to my psychologist friend, who was listening quite intently. At the right time, he turned to me and said, "I have noticed that you have not let yourself grieve all of this. You have cut yourself off from the pain. The only way to get through all of this is to dive into it. Take all that is inside and dive in to the pain, no matter how long it takes."

Looking back on that conversation now, I realize that he was advising me according to the spiritual direction of the psalms of lament. The writer of Psalm 102 begins with, "God, listen! Listen to my prayer, listen to the pain in my cries. Don't turn your back on me just when I need you so desperately. Pay attention! This is a cry for help! And hurry—this can't wait!" He is basically advising the worshipper to "dive in." Take your painful and hopeful self and give it all to this grief. Don't let decorum, self-consciousness, or guilt stand in the way of finding joy on the other side of this lament. The joy of finding our life again is initiated by the compassionate God, who weeps with us in our pain. To discover God weeping with us over the source of our grief is to find the reason to start living again. We cannot find this joy through shortcuts or by denying our pain. It only surfaces when we pray "God, listen! Listen to my prayer, listen to the pain in my cries." It is in this cry of desperation, yet hope, that the world is opened up to us. Not just to live in, but to spiritually frolic in, with joy.

---

1. Brueggemann, *Message of the Psalms*, 15–23.

Love Believes All Things

June 19, 2020

I Corinthians 13:7

[Love] bears all things, believes all things,
     hopes all things, endures all things.

THERE WERE TWO MELANCHOLY Danes in the history of Denmark, not just one. King Lear was the original melancholy Dane, brokenhearted by the deception of his daughters' false love for him. The second melancholy Dane was that philosopher of the heart, and the first psychologist of anxiety and fear, Søren Kierkegaard. His life of faith, inwardness, and commitment to the human struggle, led him into a lonely and melancholy life of servant-hood to God. He was committed to his writing, completing almost thirty books on philosophy, literature, theology, and psychology, in his short life. He wrote groundbreaking works in all areas of learning that are still relevant today. One of his works, which I read frequently, is *Works of Love*. It contains several inspirational and meditative tomes designed to help us understand the love that comes from God and how it works in the human community. One of his chapters is entitled, "Love Believes All Things—and Yet Is Never Deceived."[1]

Two of the hardest questions to accept when we open our love to another are "Will we be deceived when we do this?" and "Will we be hurt?" To believe all things seems so naïve and so dangerous. That is why Kierkegaard

1. Kierkegaard, *Works of Love*, 225–245.

adds to the statement of Paul "—and yet is never deceived." He is not saying that love can never be deceived. He means that love absorbs deception and sees the object of love as worthy, even within the possibility of deception. How many of us have fallen into this situation? One of the most famous lovers who was deceived was that first melancholy Dane, King Lear. He wanted to give each of his three daughters a share of his kingdom, if they would tell him how much they loved him. The first two daughters provided gracious attestations of their love for him, but the third, Cordelia, said, "I love you no less, or more, than a daughter should love a father." Lear was angry and took her share and gave it to the other two daughters. He believed that Cordelia was ungrateful, while his other daughters were superior in their love for him. But, in the end, he was wrong. When he learned of his two daughters' deception, he went mad. His mistake was that love should have believed Cordelia; but he was deceived by his pride.

This is what I believe Kierkegaard is getting at. Love must stand before all things and believe what the other is saying. Yet, love knows, as well, of the heart of those who are being loved. In this way, love is never deceived. It always knows the truth, because love looks to the heart. But, when love sees the heart of the other and sees that falseness is present, it doesn't mean that love is to recede. Love is to believe that the other person is worthy of love. In this, there is no deception. You may feel powerless and shameful in this kind of relationship to others, but, in truth, it is the most powerful relationship that moves the world forward.

Kierkegaard writes, "So it is with the one who loves, who believes all things. This can very easily be confused with shallowness, and yet there is the depth of wisdom in this simplicity; this can very easily be confused with weakness, and yet the powers of eternity are in this person whom anyone can deceive, and yet he is the only one who is eternally and infinitely secured against being deceived."[2] For in the end, love can never be deceived, because love knows the truth of the other. But love can be willingly deceived, albeit for a greater purpose.

---

2. Kierkegaard, *Works of Love*, 243.

The Hand of God

June 22, 2020

Hosea 6:1–4 (NIV)

Come, let us return to the Lord;

for it is he who has torn, and he will heal us;

he has struck down, and he will bind us up.

After two days he will revive us;

on the third day he will raise us up,

that we may live before him.

Let us know, let us press on to know the Lord;

his appearing is as sure as the dawn;

he will come to us like the showers,

like the spring rains that water the earth.

HOSEA IS A GREAT spiritual teacher who enters the complexities of Israel's life and pulls out the simplicity of spiritual guidance. Love is his shield against the misfortunes of life, against sin, hatred, and pain. But he not only preaches words to internalize, he preaches messages of repentance and forgiveness, coupled with dramatic actions that turn his teaching into visible representations of the hand of God. The same hand of God that tears us down is the hand that heals and revives us from God's pruning shears. Hosea dramatizes God's actions towards his people through God's request for him to marry a prostitute, and if she strays, he must forgive her and bring her back home. It is a most peculiar request, but it does exemplify what God has offered to humanity throughout history. God offers his love, even though he chastises, as well. These two actions come from the same heart and hand of our forgiving God.

Hosea makes no arguments or excuses for these actions of God. He simply recognizes them as part of the created world, part of the way God stimulates our spiritual senses to engage a complex state of affairs. Marrying a prostitute was God's way of dramatizing Israel's unfaithfulness and God's faithfulness to his promise to be their compassionate God. In this time of uncertainty, in which we feel the very heavy hand of creation's unpredictability, we need the message of Hosea. Eventually, God's pruning shears will take a rest, and the watering habits of God will be refreshing once again to us. We will once again feel the ease of walking among people, without fear. The last verses of Hosea are refreshing: "They [Israel] shall again live beneath my shadow, they shall flourish as a garden; they shall blossom like the vine, their fragrance shall be like the wine of Lebanon" (Hos 14:7–8 NIV).

The beauty of Hosea's spiritual teaching is its simplicity. Spirituality is not a quest to get things right; it is a faithful exercise of the heart, recognizing that the distractions around us create clouds of confusion. Instead of providing more light, the wayward spiritual leaders of Israel have become part of the corruption. When Hosea was asked by God to go marry a prostitute, there were probably hundreds of reasons not to do it. But, for him, it was simple. He did what God requested, in the midst of all the confusion of life. It was simple and pure, even though the woman he was marrying was not. Even the world around him, who were not pure, saw it as a disreputable act of heresy and irreligiosity. He saw God's chastisement of Israel all around him, but he chose not to make it his private complaint against Israel or God. Instead, he said I am going to love God, love my people, and love my wife. He did so by forgiving them and accepting God's request. He kept his eyes on the hand of God that tears down and heals. In this simplicity of faithfulness, he says, "Let us know, let us press on to know the Lord; his appearing is as sure as the dawn; he will come to us like the showers, like the spring rains that water the earth."

The Glory of Sharing

June 24, 2020

Philippians 2:1–2 (NEB)

If then our common life in Christ yields anything to stir the heart,

Any loving consolations, any sharing of the Spirit,

 any warmth of affection or compassion,

fill up my cup of happiness by thinking and feeling alike,

 with the same love for one another, the same turn of mind,

 and a common care for unity.

THERE IS SOMETHING LIFE-CHANGING about sharing a common purpose with others. Paul uses spiritually coated words to express how he feels towards others; when this miracle of commonality—loving consolation, compassion, happiness, and love—is acted out in the church, life changes. The commonality that he is talking about is their shared experience in Christ. You could never receive these same gifts by having a common purpose of hatred. The fruit that comes from a malevolent purpose only produces distrust, anger, and a misguided knowledge of the world and the self. To work together for a truly noble and spiritual purpose with others invites the fruits of the Spirit to release a fragrance that overwhelms the spiritual senses. Embrace, compassion, and a common care for unity provide a treasure of self-understanding that enhances the bond between all those that sense this common purpose and live it out with others.

Caring and compassion are not necessarily easily achieved human attributes. They are not necessarily endemic, either. They have to be nourished through interaction with others, for them to flourish. Community is not something that happens when people get together. It happens over time when people decide to live together for a common purpose. Paul knows this, and he hopes that the Philippian church grows into a community that finds its unity in Christ and the common purpose of preaching and demonstrating the good news. Both Paul and Jesus sacrificed their life and needs to enhance the church's ability to live in this unity. They both worked hard to provide the freedom of community that became a model for a new life in the world.

We are all looking for something to stir the heart, to jumpstart it and set it on its way. We want to step into a conscious and deliberate way of life that is shared by others. Isn't this what friendship and marriage are all about? It is our attempt to find someone with whom we can live our common dreams, all the while being filled with the excitement of being in love and loved. Paul understands that there are many roadblocks on the way to this dream. That is why he is eager to encourage the Philippian church to find this warmth of affection, compassion, and the same turn of mind. For once these fruits of friendship become mature, they are the kind of food that will sustain all of us through the tough times.

At this time in our life, it is hard to exercise these desires of unity into a visible model, given that our community is somewhat fractured by sheer distance. But we can still exercise love, warmth, and compassion with our family, all the time learning the lessons of the glory of sharing. Sharing heals the wounds of isolation. Whether it is a wave to a neighbor who is gazing at you from his or her window, or the person who walks a dog down the street, you are both dreaming of the day you can walk freely and talk to each other without distance between you. You both know the dream still exists in each of you. You both desire affection, love, and compassion, which comes from Christ. That is why we can still keep the dream alive— the glory of sharing.

Invisible Walls

June 25, 2020

Something there is that doesn't love a wall,
That sends the frozen-ground-swell under it,
And spills the upper boulders in the sun,
And makes gaps even two can pass abreast.

—ROBERT FROST[1]

THIS MORNING, MY NEIGHBOR came over to examine my floor in the bath-room that was damaged by water. When he came to the door, he reached out his hand. I immediately pulled mine back and squeezed his arm. I felt strange. Like all of us, I am used to extending my hand in friendship when someone extends theirs. There was an invisible wall that separated us, that was never there before. I immediately thought of the above Robert Frost poem, "Mending Wall," which opens with "Something there is that doesn't love a wall." I love how Frost writes the simple truth, that we do not like walls. But he doesn't state it in that way. He doesn't say "I don't like walls" as a declarative statement of fact. Instead, he writes in a more reflective and deflecting way, sending us to contemplate something deep inside us. He doesn't even necessarily write this truth in order to entice our curiosity to ponder further what it might be in us that doesn't love a wall. Frost's genius is to leave us with a haunting feeling about walls in the world: "Something there is that doesn't love a wall." What doesn't love a wall—the animals, the flowers, the river, or us? He pushes this feeling of being walled off into the

1. Frost, *Complete Poems*, 47–48.

whole of creation, as if to say, part of the human condition is the ambiguity between trying to wall ourselves off and wanting to break walls down. In fact, the last sentence of this mysterious poem reads, "Good fences make good neighbors."

We find ourselves today living in the shadow of this poem. To protect ourselves and others, we build invisible walls, which we might call "mending walls." So, the last line of the poem is as true as the first in this new world of our invisible enemy. "Good fences [do] make good neighbors," and we are good neighbors, who build walls between us. Yet, "[s]omething there is that doesn't love a wall."

It is indeed strange when, because of the changes in our world, two things so different can be true. This ambiguity is now our new reality. To help others means to wall off ourselves, yet we hate what it does to us. We are asked by the pressing destruction of this new intruder to turn our world upside down. We are forced to use our imagination in order to find ways in which walls can be porous and hard at the same time. We must make our isolation a thing of beauty for others, instead of seeing it as a punishment. We are asked to use the strange phrase "Mending Walls" as an embrace of creation, instead of thinking of walls as the things that prevent community, conversation, and togetherness. We are asked to give up our freedom, for the sake of the health of another.

There is no doubt our world is turned upside down. The one constant, however, is the voiceless voice of God, that speaks to us in the night and in the silence of our isolation. In our frustration during this upside-down world, that voice whispers to us faintly: Love, Love, Love. This is the only way to see the invisible walls between us, as Robert Frost did: "Something there is that doesn't love a wall." Yet, "[g]ood fences make good neighbors." Only love can straighten out this paradox.

Creation's Time

June 29, 2020

Genesis 1:1–3, Romans 8:20–22 (NRSV)

In the beginning when God created the heavens and the earth, the earth was a
formless void and darkness covered the face of the deep, while a wind from
God swept over the face of the waters. Then God said, "Let there be light";
and there was light.

For the creation was subjected to futility, not of its own will but by the will of the
one who subjected it, in hope that the creation itself will be set free from its
bondage to decay and will obtain the freedom of the glory of the children of
God.

Every day we wake up and think that we are living in a dream,
and things will return to our old habits of comfort very soon. We
will feel free to come out of our houses and enjoy shopping, going
to restaurants, and walking around town. We dream of feeling free
to call up friends and say, "Let's go out tonight." In other words, we
wake up to the dream that we will get back to living. But then we are
confronted with the reality that creation has put its foot down and
said, "I am taking over for a while, and you must find a way to work
with me to get back to living." This is something that we are not used

to. We don't take kindly to humbling ourselves to creation's power and will. We have felt for years, even with climate change, that we are in control. God has set creation before us as our home, with our privilege to be its gardener. But then, as history has shown, we have been mischievous children, who think we can abuse without consequence. Creation is our partner and says to us, "It is time to take care of the forces that face both of us."

We often forget that the Spirit who hovered over the earth, bringing order out of chaos in the creation story, is the same Spirit who embraces us. This Spirit comes to hover over us and within us, to direct the storms inside us that injure us and work against a partnership to establish creation's purpose. At this time, in the history of humanity, we are called again to be true partners with creation and the Spirit to help humanity establish God's purpose for "the freedom of the glory of the children of God."

What does all this mean for us every day? It means defeating the invisible enemy with love. The more we love each other, the more this army of deadly germs loses its power to infiltrate our communities. The more we respect each other, the more the enemy will be in retreat. Even the scientists' suggesting a behavior that can protect us is an act of responsibility and respect for others and creation. Masks, hand washing, social distancing are not infringements of our rights; they are an invitation to be responsible.

The more we engage in the activity of respect and hospitality, the more we will find a way to keep the enemy within its own camp. Just like racism, this is not a political issue; it is a spiritual issue. Until racism and the fighting of this invisible enemy are adopted by the church and theologians as a spiritual issue of some kind, we will not be able to fight them, in order to defeat them. Every time you stay home or keep your distance, you are partnering with the Spirit to restore creation and save the lives of others in our communities.

All communities are connected by a common purpose to thrive, but also to survive. We are connected by those things that can tear us apart, defeating our will to reach our common purpose. Fighting this virus is now the common goal of the world's communities. Unless we fight this together, our partnership will be shattered. We will have failed our neighbor, our friend, and God. Stay hopeful and stay steadfast in our quest to heal creation. Then we will witness Paul's declaration at the end of Romans 8: Nothing "will be able to separate us from the love of God" (Rom 8:39 NIV).

Cultivate Gratitude

July 1, 2020

Colossians 3:15-16

Let the peace of Christ keep you in tune with each other,
 in step with each other.
None of this going off and doing your own thing.
 And cultivate thankfulness.

PAUL SAYS IN ONE of his letters "in all things, give thanks." However, we shouldn't think he means giving thanks for evil. This would be a wrong-headed conclusion to his abundant expression of gratitude. When we look at the context in which this exuberant expression of gratitude arises in Colossians, it is about the gifts and graces God provides the church. One of those rich graces is other Christians. Paul's desire for all his churches is that they love one another with such boldness that a natural expression of gratitude arises between them, which fortifies their joint effort of doing the work of Christ. Paul is concerned that a feeling of unity and the advancement of a common purpose be embraced within the church. An equal submission to each other, in the spirit of love, is required to withstand the forces of division that would derail their common venture.

Gratitude is such a difficult expression to define. It is mainly used, in Christian communities, to explain our intentions to give something back to God. Worship is, and always has been, hands and eyes lifted to the sky, in order to say "thank you." Worship is gratitude. It is that singular expression of worship, letting God know that we appreciate the love, gifts, purpose, and peace that come from his wisdom and heart. Gratitude is the lifting up of our love to God, to express our feeling of appreciation for the gifts we have been given. When my child was born, my thought and my desire was to give thanks to God for this unworthy gift. In the same way, a friend of mine, who is not a believer in God, told me that when his child was born, he wished that he believed, so he could say "thank you." So, gratitude is mostly associated with an expression of receiving something you feel unworthy to be given and honored to be its recipient. It is a way of harnessing our appreciation in words and feelings.

Paul uses this most sacred word to tell his congregation to be thankful recipients of each other. He wants them to contemplate the commensurate gifts they are to each other. He desires they be grateful for one another, recognizing that they are special gifts in their life. Even when they drive you crazy, they help carve a sculptured personality that is learning to live in the presence of God. When that is accepted as a necessary piece of spiritual development, we will have lived out the purpose of God and Paul. The acceptance of one another is a heart growing in the Spirit, who has taken all the trials of life and turned them into a word that we cannot live without: hope. Hope and gratitude cannot exist without each other. For when we say "thank you," we are saying at the same time "I have power to persist until the end."

"There are only two ways to live your life. One is as though nothing is a miracle. The other is as though everything is a miracle," says Albert Einstien.[1] Another way to say this is: "There are only two ways to live your life. One is to give thanks for all the gifts that have made you, you. The other is to suggest that life is life, and has no special gifts." One leads to hope and gratitude' the other leads to a loss of engagement with others and, most importantly, with God. It is most important during this time of isolation to embrace the former. Give thanks, be grateful for what you have now, instead of thinking that all the good and bad of the past is just part of life. It is more than that. It is the good soil in which we were grown, and others are part of that good soil.

1. Although this quote did not appear in print, others have attested to its validity in Einstien's informal conversation.

The Mirror of Christ

July 3, 2020

"Exactly in the same sense St. Francis is nearer to us,

and being mere man like ourselves is in that sense more imaginable [than

Christ]."

—*G.K. Chesterton*[1]

It is fair to say that probably no one in the history of Christianity lived his or her faith more clearly than St. Francis. G.K. Chesterton, that great master of stories, suggests that St. Francis lived a life so close to Christ's that the mysteries that seem to surround Jesus's teaching are mere paradoxes in the life of St. Francis. In other words, while Christ was divine and St. Francis mortal, St. Francis was able to open up many of the mysteries of Jesus's teaching just by living a simple life for Christ. It is notorious that he gave away everything he owned and lived off the goodness of others. Many called him the "little beggar." But this was not a derogatory slur. He was beloved by all, for he was kind in his preaching and not judgmental. Along with his simple life, he was also a builder. Because of his love for all creatures, both human and animal, he was able to attract a great many people to his lifestyle. Chesterton calls him one of the greatest "builders" of community produced in Christianity and one of the most equitable. He was the first leader to allow women into his community, which brought forth one of the most delightful individuals of that period, Clare. She was

---

1. Chesterton, *St. Francis*, 173.

so admired for her love and gentleness that the pope made a special trip to speak at her funeral.

One of the simple pleasures of this isolation, during our unfortunate visitor, is to be able to catch up on my reading. Besides reading poetry, I have also started reading some of the great mystics and spiritual giants of Christianity. St. Francis is just one of many where I have found solace, not for his teaching, of which there is very little, but for the stories of his life. Francis was adamant that he should not leave any documents about his teaching, fearing that some would revere the document itself and not see behind it. Most of what we know about him and his teaching was written down by his disciples. Much like Jesus, who wrote nothing of which we know, Francis spent his time living and not documenting. Like Jesus, what Francis left us was a magnificent treasury of stories told about him by devoted followers. He left no organized theology, nor an organizing principle of how to live in faith. He simply showed everyone. That was his genius.

We all wonder, at times, how will people remember us. Einstein is remembered for creating the formula for the atom bomb and also helping us define the nature of the universe. But do we remember his great works in politics, designed to bring the world together in peace? St. Francis was worried that he would be remembered through the documents of his spiritual insights, instead of showing people how to live. The world chooses to remember events and the character of people for their own reasons, but it may not be the reasons they want to be remembered. Francis made sure how to be remembered. He knew human nature and our desire for a hero would skew some of his unique purpose in life. He chose not to be a hero, but a "little beggar" for Christ.

Isolation does not prevent us from being "mirrors of Christ." The only thing that prevents us from this spiritual purpose is being caught up in the desires and fears of the world. St. Francis conquered his fear of leprosy in order to care for all the diseased people in the world. Conquering our fear of death is a way to live with and for Christ with abandon. When we are able to be free of this, we will be able to follow Christ in the same kind of simplicity as St. Francis. Then we will be remembered for what is the most precious thing we have created: a life of faith.

COVID-19 Impact

July 6, 2020

2 Corinthians 5:18–19 (NRSV)

All this is from God, who reconciled us to himself through Christ, and has given us the ministry of reconciliation; that is, in Christ God was reconciling the world to himself, not counting their trespasses against them, and entrusting the message of reconciliation to us.

EVERY WEEK, I SIT down to write these meditations, hoping and praying for direction. I hope to put words together that will have some expressive purpose, that what I write might enhance understanding and spiritual challenges. I desire to give shape to some spiritual vision that comes from God. As I sat down today, starring at an empty screen, I realized how tired I am. I am tired of the monotony, the constant caution that surrounds us, and the tediousness of the ministry to which all pastors are resigned, in this season of life. But then it dawned on me: we are all in the same boat, floating on a tranquil sea, going nowhere. There is an equality of experience that opens my heart to empathy. I know what you feel, and you know what I feel. We no longer need to feel hollow when we say "I know how you feel," when we really don't. We all know how each of us feels. We have wrapped ourselves in hope, looking through a glass darkly, picking ourselves up every day to turn sameness into an adventure. But it is not the adventure that makes us tired, it is the sameness.

When I talk to people throughout the week, I feel their burden and mine. This is where our empathy is forged, in the gloominess of the days behind and ahead of us. Within the tussle of remembering and fearing what is ahead, there is hope. It is also where the adventure of these days is forged. These thoughts remind me of that famous line in *King Lear*, when Lear seems to be going mad, but his empathy is expanding. He says, "Expose thyself to feel what wretches feel, / That thou mayst shake the superflux to them, / And show the heavens more just."[1] Lear is actually preaching to us. He wants us to expose ourselves to the pain of others, to become more empathetic, in order to bring equality and care to the world, as well as a little more kindness. Each of us has the opportunity to indulge ourselves in this meeting of hearts. It is what unites us and solidifies our identity in the communities we live. But there is one more way in which we are united, sharing an equality with each other. Paul provides this insight in 2 Corinthians 5:19, saying, "[I]n Christ God was reconciling the world to himself, not counting their trespasses against them, and entrusting the message of reconciliation to us." As part of the world, God was reconciling us through the death and resurrection of Jesus. We all share in his death, even if we don't share the experience of believing in its efficacy. It is still a kindness delivered to all who live in the world. Through seeing the kindness in this sacrificial reconciliation, we have become equal partners in the extension of God's grace. So, when we encounter people on the street, in stores and all the places in the world, we are to acknowledge that "God is reconciling them to himself." We have empathy for both those who believe in this reconciliation and those who don't. The reason it is convincing is because it was done with and for love. Therefore, this sacrifice can produce empathy for others, even if it is not faithfully acknowledged, as a gift of God. In this regard, we are called to feel the weight of being kind to others.

COVID-19 has given us a common burden to carry for each other, and, in exchange, God has given us a common bond, as well. We are the recipients of God's reconciling work. This is our adventure, and it defeats the tediousness of life that wants to drag us down by drowning us in a sea of sameness. But it doesn't have to. Empathy expands the mind and heart to the good will of others; thus comes the wind, pulling us forward.

1. Shakespeare, *King Lear*, 84.

Life Is Messy

July 8, 2020

"I am a man
More sinned against than sinning."

—SHAKESPEARE, *KING LEAR*, *ACT III*, *SCENE 2*

"O do you dread
My strength? My actions? I think not, for I
Suffered those deeds more than I acted them."

—SOPHOCLES, *OEDIPUS AT COLONUS*, *LINES 265–68*

I PAIRED THESE QUOTES because both playwrights use the same idea to describe the brokenness of their protagonists. Sophocles, more than a thousand years before Shakespeare, wrote his immortal words describing the misfortune that came upon Oedipus. Oedipus was taken up to the mountains to die as a baby, because of a prophecy stating that he would kill his father, King Laius, and marry his mother, Queen Jocasta of Thebes. But King Polybus and Queen Merope found the child and raised him as their own in Corinth. Oedipus finds out about the prophecy and leaves home for Thebes, in order to protect his parents. On the road to Thebes he is attacked by his real father King Laius and kills him, thus fulfilling the prophecy. Oedipus remains in Thebes and becomes an honored and courageous man. He eventually marries Queen Jocasta, thereby completing the prophecy. All this is done in ignorance.

In the intervening years, discovering what he has done, he removes his eyes and begins to wander throughout Greece. It is in Colonus that he says before the heavens and the people there, "O do you dread my strength? My actions? I think not, for I suffered those deeds more than I acted them." The calamity that comes upon him, he believes, is not of his doing, but was a misfortune of life that was unjustly punished by the gods.

Lear has a similar outlook on his life. What happened to him was unjustified and cruel. His two daughters saw him as an arrogant fool and threw him out of his own kingdom, when they seized power. We can see links with these two characters and Job's fight for justice as well. Job could say, along with his two brothers in suffering, "I am a man more sinned against than sinning." Some might say that they were all arrogant and should have just accepted their fate, given that life itself is not fair. But there is something inside us that doesn't like injustice. So, we demand it, especially from our divine powers—Oedipus from Zeus, Lear from God, and Job from God, as well.

There is no better place in our Scripture to work this paradox out than the psalms. While many of the psalms sing with praise and joy, most of them are working things out in a messy world. There is the recurring cry of pain in the words "How long, Lord, will you continually punish me, or forget me." There is the constant shaking of the fist against God's inactivity. These are just a few recurring expressions of frustration and pain that arise from a life that seems to have little justice. The psalms are not in themselves the resolution to this messy world. They are the road map to the only one who can provide a way to navigate this messy life: Christ. After expunging our emotions, through the agonizing expression of anger and frustration, what is left for us to do but to fall on our knees and listen in silence to the heavenly wisdom of Christ? We may never come to a resolution about why certain things happen to us. Lear, Oedipus, and Job couldn't find it on their own. Job found peace, but only after being exhausted through theological conversations with his friends, then finding God in a whirlwind. The only reasonable action was to watch and listen. He needed to experience his anger and melt before the incendiary presence of God.

God's Light Is Our Refuge

July 9, 2020

Psalm 27:1-2 (NEB)

The Lord is my light and my salvation.

I fear no one.

The Lord protects my life.

I am afraid of no one.

When evil men attack me

to devour my flesh,

when my adversaries and enemies attack me,

they stumble and fall.

PSALM 27 IS WRITTEN by a spiritual master who is in love with God. The psalmist is completely united with God, who has embraced him by the power of love. Therefore, he feels completely protected from evil or anything that can harm him. In fact, the psalmist feels so protected that he believes that when those who dabble in evil come against him, they will be the ones who will fall, not him. It is as if he is surrounded by an invisible force shield of love that protects him, but does no harm to others. The only harm that comes to those that dabble in evil is the failure to penetrate this invisible force shield that God provides, therefore rendering inoperative their design to turn God's children towards an evil design in the world, instead of a holy one.

It is psalms like this that gave rise to mystics throughout the eleventh and twelfth centuries, mystics like Bernard of Clairvaux. Bernard gave us sermons, meditations, and theological reflections that were all designed to help the lover of God to grow deeper into a spiritual relationship with the divine God. It was common for these mystics to use the Song of Songs to express their relationship with God. As you are aware, this is the story of two lovers, expressing their love for each other. Bernard sees in this love story the story of himself and God. While it may seem inappropriate to use the words of lovers to shape a meditation about our relationship with God, Bernard takes delight in using these expressions, since he believes that love is what binds us to God. In one of his meditations on the Song of Songs, he says, "If you are holy, you are understood and known. If not, be holy and you will know by experience. Holy affection makes a holy person and it is twofold—holy fear of God and holy love. The soul that is perfectly affected by these two, like twin arms, grasps, embraces, binds, holds fast and says, 'I have held him and will not let him go.'"[1]

He is describing a marriage experience, which he believes translates to his fellowship with God. His words have the same sentiment that we find in Psalm 27. Both Bernard and the psalmist are enraptured by the object of their love, and they feel protected and safe in the arms of their lover. For Bernard, as well as the psalmist, experience is the source of their knowledge of love. They do not love from a distance or through some kind of admiration. They love through desire, the desire to know the other in the fullness of all that is in them. Both of these great spiritual giants are contemplative masters, seeking visions of how God walks among creation, to establish hope, care, and the future of love.

While it is difficult to maintain this kind of intensity, it is reassuring that at times, and especially during these desperate times, God is waiting with open arms. This is "my light and my salvation." God is my salvation from despair and my light to see through the distractions of fear. This experience is open to me when I understand, like Bernard, "I have held him and will not let him go."

1. McGinn, *Growth of Mysticism*, 207.

God Is the Sun

July 13, 2020

Isaiah 60:19–20 (NEB)

The sun will no longer supply light for you by day,
nor will the moon's brightness shine on you;
the Lord will be your permanent source of light—
the splendor of your God will shine upon you.
Your sun will no longer set;
your moon will not disappear;
the Lord will be your permanent source of light;
your time of sorrow will be over.

IN THE DOG DAYS of summer, there is a tendency to stay in our homes, so as to not be scorched by the heat, which surely dulls the senses. But during these strange days of COVID-19, we are already planted in our homes and see the sun as a welcome light to our shadowy existence. By now, we are growing accustomed to this new way of life into which we were forced and at the same time chose, in order to heal and save each other. We have taken on new habits, slowed down a bit, learned to arrange our life with each other, so as to make life interesting. Some of us are finding it exhausting. Others are welcoming the forced demand to slow down. But still the sun beckons us to come out and enjoy the light and the heat, providing us with a welcome distraction.

Anyone who has spent time in Isaiah knows what a wonderful poet he is—a prophet with a talent for introducing God with words that cut like swords and penetrate our hardened hearts. Chapter sixty of Isaiah has long been a favorite of the synagogues and churches. It contains promises to Israel which are not apparent at the time of its writing, but provide a welcomed hope to those who cannot see God in their present situation. The following sentence quickens the heart, providing hope for the believer: "The sun will no longer supply light for you by day, nor will the moon's brightness shine on you; the Lord will be your permanent source of light— the splendor of your God will shine upon you. Your sun will no longer set; your moon will not disappear; the Lord will be your permanent source of light; your time of sorrow will be over.

He presents the hope of Israel through the metaphor of light. Humanity depends upon the sun and moon for perception and many other things, like growing crops and the natural heat to shield against the cold. But instead of using this reality to show God's providence and care, he diminishes this reality of sun and moon to create another one. God is now our light, our sun and moon. By doing this, he is relegating what we might think is the most important light to a secondary place. Spiritual light is more necessary to life than the sun and moon. God has taken over the role of the sun, which is needed for survival. To enjoy this sun and dance within its light is our way of renewing our life every day. God brightens the room and all its inhabitants in the same way that God brightens the world with a light that comes through his Word and heart. Anything other than this amounts to a path not worth taking. But we usually don't understand this until the end of the journey. Isaiah is our prophet of vision and spiritual understanding of what is important in life. What is important for Isaiah is to convince us that God is the new sun and moon, and that is all we need.

As we are resting in our homes, during this time of isolation, it may be hard to convince ourselves that all we need is what Isaiah has preached. We need not look beyond our walls and be drawn by the heat and light of the sun, which, of course, is helpful to us. But it can't create the joy of the light of God. Isaiah wants us to dance in our homes. He wants us to learn caring and compassion with those who share our four walls—loving consolation, compassion, happiness, and love. He wants us to learn to be alone with God, before we step into the light of the day, to be with others.

The Pain of Fear

July 15, 2020

Zygmunt Baumann, that prophet of modernism and postmodernism, describes in his and Leonidas Donskis's book *Moral Blindness: The Loss of Sensitivity in Liquid Modernity* that there are three reasons to be afraid in our modern world. The first is ignorance—not knowing what is going to happen and fearing the worst. The second reason is powerlessness—not knowing what is going to happen and not being able to do anything about it. Finally, we are afraid we will be humiliated for not doing all we could do in the time given us, to help humanity.[1] Each one of these reasons to be afraid carries its own pain. There is the pain that surrounds the unknown in our life, which we bury within the distractions of daily living. The fear of the unknown creates a pain of being off-balance and wary of investing too much because we are so unsure. The pain we call "unsureness" can only be healed by entering into the swirl of life and allowing it to take us forward. Trying to control this fear through distractions only increases the pain, which paralyzes us from moving anywhere.

The second reason to fear is a deepening of the first. It is one thing to fear the future because we don't know what is going to happen; it is another to feel the powerlessness that stops us from any action. While the first (unknowing) creates the pain of being unsure of ourselves and life, the second reason (powerlessness) creates the pain of profound shame. Shame always arises in the awareness of our powerlessness. Shame creates pain in us because it tells us that we are weak. The only way we can move

---

1. Bauman and Donskis, *Moral Blindness*, 96–108.

beyond this pain is to take action against the fear. In the same way that the second reason to fear is a deepening of the first, the third is a deepening of the second. By Bauman and Donskis suggesting that we are afraid of being humiliated for not doing enough for others, they are moving past the pain of shame to the core of our self-identity. When we lose the ability to understand our legacy in the world, we experience the pain of becoming invisible. Yes, there is shame, yes, there is unsureness, but there is also the pain that we will be forgotten. It is the pain associated with the fear that we have nothing to give; therefore, we are, in a sense, just taking up space.

So why do I mention all these pains and fears? Mainly because they are my fears and pains. I wonder at times, have I done enough. I wonder if I have helped. But most of this is associated with what I see others doing and feel I am so far behind doing my fair share in this world of our invisible enemy. It is always dangerous to compare ourselves with what others do. Most of us are not good at this exercise. We tend to exaggerate on either side of the coin. This only increases the problem, which in the end is our paralysis in the face of this overwhelming crisis. Most of us have a bit of the heroic in us. We want to overcome these fears and step into the mess of the world. As we do, we hope to make a difference. When we feel we haven't, there enters the pain that continues to stop us from doing anything.

For me, I have come to accept the limitations of being able to do all the things I wish I could do for others. Right now, I understand the most I can do is to be your pastor and to write helpful articles and provide sermons that might stimulate a desire to seek a deeper relationship with God. I have found that accepting our limitations and working within them is a way of carving out a meaningful life. Strangely, it is also a way of diminishing the pain of my fears. The lesson of this crisis is "just do something" that you can for others and thus diminish the power of these fears in our life. At the same time, know that you are entering into the life of the world, becoming real and visible for others.

Comfort, Comfort My People

July 17, 2020

Isaiah 40:1–2 (NEB)

"Comfort, comfort my people,"
says your God.
"Speak kindly to Jerusalem and tell her
that her time of warfare is over, that her punishment is completed.
For the Lord has made her pay double, for all her sins."

As I CONTEMPLATE WHAT I will work on during my time away, my thoughts move to all of you. There isn't a day that I do not think of what it means to be a pastor and especially your pastor. I can't help myself, because that is what I am—a pastor. I am a person driven by God to care for others, teach and carry burdens, whenever I am capable. At least that is my calling. Isaiah was a pastor as well. His words, whether they sting or heal, are draped with the colorful shades of beauty that, when you visualize them, are comforting in their symmetry. In chapter forty of his work, he hears the admonition from God "Comfort, comfort my people." This is what they need. They have been through the fires, the stinging tragedy of war and economic destitution. They have also been separated from their country, being held captive by those that wanted their land and money. Through this they have experienced their sin and its consequences. It is time now to build a new life. But they need encouragement and comfort to make it through the hard work. They need a pastor like Isaiah.

This is the background for Isaiah's work and all pastors', really. It is a work that is so important for Isaiah and pastors everywhere. We need to deal with our own disappointment, anger, and sin, before moving into that sacred interior of others. In other words, we need to let the comfort of God shower us with encouragement before we attempt the calming in others. It would be wrong for Isaiah or any pastor to inflict the pain of weakness on others. It is impossible to be of any help if we do not go through the training as a comforter—which means we must first bind our wounds, so that we do not infect others with our contagious ooze of sin and arrogance.

Not just anyone can provide meaningful comfort to others. There is a way of knowing others, visualizing their pain and placing yourself within the context of their lives. If we miss this, then we have missed the opportunity of standing in for God to provide the calm and hope that provides a spiritual embrace in others.

Isaiah was commanded by God to "speak kindly to Jerusalem." It doesn't mean that he must withhold the truth. Rather, he is commanded to speak with a certain poise that comes from knowing what his country needs. What Israel needs are words that can empower them to build their nation again. What we need are words that lift us up to continue to organize, plan, and believe that God is still with us through this crisis. We need to believe that this invisible enemy will not defeat us. When we believe this, there is our comfort.

The wonderful gift that is provided by the Spirit is the power to administer mercy to others. We are called, no matter if we are a professional pastor or a spiritual pastor of the community. The pastorate is not housed in one person in the community. It is disseminated to everyone. In this way, we all have to go through a training to be comforters. We must let God comfort us within the sin and misery of our life. Then we will be ready. Binding our wounds is a learning experience of grace. Isaiah was a man who became a great spiritual leader, because he did just that. He patiently worked through the wounds of his life, because of God and Israel, which gave him the insight into what others need and ability to find hope in their life. In this respect, Jesus is our comfort, because he reveals his wounds, which allows us to bind the wounds of others.

Further Reading

Bauman, Zygmunt. *Community: Seeking Safety in an Insecure World.* Cambridge, UK: Polity Press, 2001.

———. *Liquid Fear.* Cambridge, UK: Polity Press, 2006.

Bauman, Zygmunt, and Leonidas Donskis. *Moral Blindness: The Loss of Sensitivity in Liquid Modernity.* Cambridge, UK: Polity Press, 2013.

Professor Bauman has become a man of clarity during this twenty-first century. His series on "Liquid Modernity" has established him as a sociologist of outstanding quality. His work is helping us come to grips with the nuances of this century. His titles suggest that individuals and communities in this century are going through a tremendous vulnerability that needs to be accepted before we can move beyond our loss of security.

Berry, Wendell. *The Art of the Common Place: The Agrarian Essays of Wendell Berry.* Edited by Norman Wirzba. Washington, D.C.: Counterpoint: 2003.

———. *Home Economics: Fourteen Essays.* San Francisco: North Point, 1987.

Wendel Berry is one of our national treasurers, who through his simple style and ideas has become a profound force for change. His life moves into his politics, and his politics defines his life style. He is in all respects a complete person, beating his own drum, but with a beat that proclaims deep spirituality.

Bonhoeffer, Dietrich. *The Cost of Discipleship.* Translated by R.H. Fuller, revised by Irmgard Booth. 2nd ed. New York: Macmillan Co., 1959.

Ethics. Edited by Eberhard Bethge, translated by N.H. Smith. 2nd ed. London: SCM Press, 1955.

Letters and Papers from Prison. Edited by Eberhard Bethge. Rev. ed. New York: Touchstone, 1997.

As one of the significant theological change makers of the twentieth century, Bonhoeffer has become synonymous with the phrase: "Only the suffering God can help." While not giving up the sovereignty of God, he introduces us to the vulnerable God, who takes on the pain of the world. In his time as well as ours, this profound understanding of God is a helpful instrument in this time of suffering and fear.

Bruce, F.F. *Paul: Apostle of the Heart Set Free.* Grand Rapids: Eerdmans, 1977.

Of all the books on Paul that I have read, this one carries with it a true efficiency of insight and a passionate quest for the apostle's love for Jesus. In all the chapters, you feel Bruce's love for Paul and how Paul reveals his love for Jesus. This book is more than a travelogue about Paul's building of churches. It is a heartfelt tribute to a man that changed the world. Worthy reading for beginners and scholars alike. He brings alive what is possible, in even the worst of times.

Brueggemann, Walter. *The Message of the Psalms: A Theological Commentary.* Augsburg Old Testament Studies. Minneapolis: Augsburg, 1985.

When we enter the psalms, we often find them difficult, because there is not one uniform theme that emerges. Brueggemann provides a useful tool to help us read the psalms without giving up. He suggests that the psalms have three kinds of themes: orientation, disorientation, and new orientation. Psalms of orientation usually connect us to worship and to the goodness of God. Psalms of disorientation have usually been called laments; they connect us to the deep pain of the emptiness of life. Finally, psalms of new orientation are those connecting us out of the regular and the painful to a hope beyond what we can see. This is a useful guide to the spiritual traveler during these times.

Buechner, Frederick. *Telling the Truth: The Gospel as Tragedy, Comedy, and Fairy Tale.* San Francisco: Harper & Row, 1977.

In typical style, Beuchner finds another side to the story of life. In the pain, he can find comedy; in the tragedies, he can find joy. In this, he finds several ways of "telling the truth" about the gospel that bring the story of our spiritual journey alive. This is a delightful book whose title is influenced by Emily Dickinson's great poem "Tell All the Truth but Tell It Slant." Buechner has learned his lesson well.

Chesterton, G.K. *St. Francis of Assisi*. New York: George H. Doran Co., 1924.

Chesterton is known mainly for his novels and prose, most recently for the character of Father Brown, who was a crime-fighting clergyman. Here, in his book on St. Francis, he paints a picture of a complex yet simple man, who was a troubadour and poet for God. Francis was also a builder of community and lover of all creation. Chesterton does not chronicle his life as much as expose it to the world for all to enjoy. There are many lessons to be learned by Francis, but the one needed today is "learn to live in poverty with joy."

Derrida, Jacques. *The Gift of Death*. Translated by David Wills. Chicago: University of Chicago Press, 1995.

The name of Jacques Derrida may not be known to many readers, but to the readers of philosophy he is known as a pioneer. He is known to have invented the method and process we now call "deconstruction" and led the world of academics into the perspective known as "postmodern." Here in this small book he tackles religion. He does approach it as an insider, but as an observer of the importance of religion. He says, "If religion means anything, it means responsibility." He sees this as religion's most important contribution to the world: responsibility to the world and each other.

Dickinson, Emily. *The Complete Poems of Emily Dickinson*. Edited by Thomas H. Johnson. Boston: Little, Brown and Company, 1960.

During a world crisis, like this pandemic, it is important to attach your feelings to words that can inspire you and identify you. Poets are usually the best vehicles we have for this. Emily Dickinson is one of the best at helping us to access our isolation and pain. I have found her helpful during this time. She is definitely worth going back to again and again.

Eliot, T.S. *The Complete Poems and Plays*. New York: Harcourt, Brace & World, 1952.

I don't believe there is any other poet who captured the world of World War I and its aftermath as clearly as T.S. Eliot. His early poems, such as "The Love Song of J. Alfred Prufrock," are filled with words of paralysis created by fear and trauma, such as "yellow fog" and "In a minute there is time / For decisions and revisions which a minute will reverse." And then there is the famous phrase, "Do I dare / Disturb the universe?" His poems are helpful to hear in a time like ours, teetering on paralysis.

Eagleton, Terry. *Hope without Optimism*. Page-Barbour Lectures. Charlottesville, VA: University of Virginia Press, 2015.

———. *On Evil*. New Haven, CT: Yale University Press, 2010.

———. *Sweet Violence: The Idea of the Tragic*. Oxford: Wiley-Blackwell, 2003.

This quirky philosopher has become one of my favorite people to read. He seems to take you down one path, to a logical conclusion, and then pulls the rug out from under you. I like it. He is erudite, wise, and funny. But, of course, he is Irish. His books are not just about academic pursuits, but are heavily paved with the stuff of real life and especially religion.

Einstein, Albert. *Ideas and Opinions*. Edited by Carl Seelig, translated and revised by Sonja Bargmann. New York: Crown Publishers, 1954.

In this collection of essays, Einstein shares his thoughts on morality, religion, politics, and the responsibility of science. After reading this collection, you will come to the conclusion that if the world had listened to him, peace would be much closer at hand. I commend these essays that are accessible and clear about the prospects of living in a world of fear and insecurity.

Frost, Robert. *Complete Poems of Robert Frost*. New York: Holt, Rinehart and Winston, 1964.

Robert Frost is no abstract poet, trying to confuse you. He is a concrete poet who describes what he sees around him, then uses it for lessons and the harsh realities of life. You won't find a lot of hope in his poems, but you will find the truth about things. Even his famous poem "The Road Not Taken" is not a hopeful poem. It is a challenge. But he cannot tell you where this road will go, or, by taking it, how it will affect you. Because of this, he paints a life that is a mystery and can be harsh.

Havel, Václav. *The Art of the Impossible: Politics as Morality in Practice*. Translated by Paul Wilson et al. New York: Alfred A. Knopf, 1997.

———. *Open Letters: Selected Writings 1965–1990*. Edited by Paul Wilson. 11th ed. New York: Vintage Books, 1992.

Václav Havel is one of those once-in-a-lifetime prophets and thinkers who is pushed into a position of power, but never abuses it. He was a playwright, philosopher, and thinker of all things human. That entails politics, religion, and morality. After being put in prison by the Communist party in Czechoslovakia for his decedent writings and speeches, he was released. In 1990, he became the first democratically elected president in Czechoslovakia. His speeches are direct and filled with possibility, but not without condemnation. These two books are worth reading for their striking sense of caring for humanity and their spiritual direction to try to change the world.

Kierkegaard, Søren. *Works of Love*. Edited and translated by Howard V. Hong and Edna H. Hong. Kierkegaard's Writings 16. Princeton, NJ: Princeton University Press, 1995.

One could spend a lifetime reading Kierkegaard's Philosophical Fragments *and still not come to a complete conclusion. The same can be said regarding* Unscientific Postscript to the Philosophical Fragments. *But while these are seemingly inaccessible, his spiritual writings are uplifting and helpful.* Works of Love *is one of his spiritual writings from which I often glean. His works seem to be suited for a troubled time, such as ours. His chapter on "Love Believes All Things—and Yet Is Never Deceived," is one of the most thoughtful and meaningful writings on Paul's paragraphs in 1 Corinthians 13.*

Lear, Jonathan. *Radical Hope: Ethics in the Face of Cultural Devastation*. Cambridge, MA: Harvard University Press, 2008.

Here is one of the most insightful and inspiring books I have read in a while. Jonathan Lear takes us on a journey of the life of Plenty Coups (1848–1932), the last great leader of the Crow Nation. During the uprisings of the Sioux against the military, Plenty Coups put down his arms and said, "No more war." Much of this was because of a dream he had, which was really a prophecy of the death of the Crow, if they continued this path of destruction. In this fascinating story of how he turned his tribe from being defined as warriors to farmers, Lear tells us that he was able to save a nation, while providing it a new vision for life. You will find this book useful in these troubled times, in which destruction and despair are replaced by a "radical hope."

McGinn, Bernard. *The Growth of Mysticism*. New York: Crossroad, 1994.

Twelfth-century mystics are identified mainly with exploring love in all its respects, both human and divine. They saw stories in the Bible as instruments to attach their understanding of God to human emotions. *Bernard of Clairvaux was a mystic of love. Although not the only one to use the Song of Songs (a love story in the Old Testament) for our relationship with God, he explored it to its depth. His sermons on the Song of Songs are almost romantic in their tone, but filled with honor and obedience to God as holy, as well. McGinn is a foremost expert on these mystics and their building up of the church. He finds in Bernard, especially, a dogged persistence to capture God's love for human beings and how we can climb the ladder to find it.*

Milosz, Czeslaw. *Selected Poems: 1931–2004.* New York: Harper Collins, 2006.

When one hears the name Milosz, one usually thinks of The Captive Mind. *That wonderful book details the events of fascist Germany and the rise of communism through a fiction that is powerful and imaginative. It is indeed a groundbreaking work for anyone living in the communist Poland of the 1950s. But I have been more fascinated with his poems, many of them reflecting the suffering of those living under communism. The ones I am reading now are from his later period, which capture the feelings of the world at the beginning of the twenty-first century. I particularly like his short poem entitled "If There Is No God." Here is a deeply sensitive man who finds spirituality in the everyday life of people.*

Nouwen, Henri J.M. *The Inner Voice of Love: A Journey through Anguish and Freedom.* New York: Random House, 1999.

———. *The Wounded Healer: Ministry in Contemporary Society.* New York: Image, 1979.

Henri J.M. Nouwen was indeed one of the most recognizable people in the world of spirituality and community life. In these two books he addresses both topics. In The Inner Voice of Love, *he reveals his secret diaries from a time in his life when he was deeply depressed. He had lost himself and was reaching out to God. I love these meditations for the genuineness and heartfelt love for humanity, while he tried to reach inside himself. These two quests collide to create the wisdom that love brings to all of us.* The Wounded Healer *takes us into the inner workings of community. It is a journey into sacrifice and kindness. In this time of suffering, we need his wisdom to navigate the life of the Spirit.*

Patočka, Jan. *Body, Community, Language, World.* Edited by James Dodd, translated by Erazim Kohák. Chicago: Open Court, 1998.

―――. *Heretical Essays in the Philosophy of History.* Edited by James Dodd, translated by Erazim Kohák. Chicago: Open Court, 1996.

Many will find these volumes impenetrable. That is unfortunate given the insights that are contained in them. While his language may be of that of a philosopher talking to other academics, it is worth the journey to catch a few morsels of clear insight, especially about how religion is so important for the establishment of freedom. This Czech philosopher is without parallel among his contemporaries. In every movement of freedom, he finds the lost quest for opening up the human spirit. I hope that those who have the desire to read patiently these remarkable paragraphs of hope during a troubled time will take the time to do so.

Paz, Octavio. *The Poems of Octavio Paz.* Edited and translated by Eliot Weinberger. New York: New Directions, 1990.

Octavio Paz was a Mexican poet with the all the gifts of imagery, comedy, and the romantic associated with Mexican authors. But his unusual gift is hi connection with the natural world, which in some ways has political import. His poetry, while interested in the natural, weaves a web of excitement for life. His propensity toward hope is exhilarating for the reader. "A Draft of Shadows" is a spellbinding poem that captures the joy and hope of the world, under the light of the sun. What a great poem to read during this time of isolation.

Peterson, Eugene H. *Answering God: The Psalms as Tools for Prayer.* San Francisco: Harper SanFrancisco, 1991.

―――. *A Long Obedience in the Same Direction: Discipleship in an Instant Society.* Downers Grove, IL: InterVarsity Press, 1980.

No one can escape the name of Eugene Peterson when they start looking for a Bible to read. His translation entitled The Message *has now become a well-known fixture in churches and homes all over the world. But before this monumental work, Eugene Peterson was writing books for pastors and lay people. Most of his books concern the psalms. His book* Answering God *helps readers navigate the psalms and helps them see the contours of the language and feelings attached to them. Many of us have problems with the language of hate and the term "enemy." We think of God as love, which makes it hard to attach these negative feelings to God. We think them dishonorable. But*

Eugene Peterson takes on a ride through our true feelings, with these psalms, and helps us come out more spiritual on the other side. It is a useful book in times of social division and turmoil.

Shakespeare, William. *Hamlet*. Edited by Burton Raffel. Annotated Shakespeare Series. New Haven, CT: Yale University Press, 1963.

———. *King Lear*. Edited by Burton Raffel. Annotated Shakespeare Series. New Haven, CT: Yale University Press, 1966.

Who doesn't know the line "To be, or not to be"? Or the great line from King Lear *"Poor naked wretches . . . that bide the pelting of this pitiless storm." Shakespeare takes troubled people and troubled times and makes them into a play for humanity. Both* Hamlet *and* King Lear *are true tragedies. But within them are lessons and insights about life. We find that both rise above their suffering to portray a deeper human compassion. Isn't that what we all want in these times—compassion?*

Sophocles. *The Complete Greek Tragedies*. Edited and translated by David Grene, edited by Richard Lattimore. Modern Library 3. New York: Random House, 1953.

*Who has not heard of the Oedipus complex or the tragedy of Oedipus himself, who married his mother in ignorance? Sophocles, author of this story, tries to tell the story of all human experience. The Greeks were no strangers to understanding life as a fateful existence, driven by the whims of the gods. This was their explanation of why bad things happen to good people. At the same time, they understood "hubris" (arrogance) as another explanation of why people fall into the devastation of guilt. The three plays contained in this volume—*Antigone, Oedipus the King, *and* Oedipus at Colonus—*tell the story of how the law and the goodness of love collide to create tragedy. This is all to say that life is messy. Its mess is contained within ignorance and hubris, which drive us away from solving our problems.*

Tocqueville, Alexis de. *Democracy in America*. 2 vols. New York: Vintage Books, 1990.

There is probably no need to write something on this work. It is the backbone of all historians' writing on the beginnings and character of our democracy. This Frenchman has captured the American character and American problems. He laid bare our weaknesses and challenges. The second volume on responsibility versus freedom is worthy reading. In this world, when we are calling for responsibility, we are hearing the response by many, "no thanks." This constant struggle will forever be the paradox that defines our future.

Wright, N.T. *God and the Pandemic: A Christian Reflection on the Coronavirus and Its Aftermath.* Grand Rapids: Zondervan, 2020.

I received this book just after finishing my own. With his usual dispatch, Wright takes on the topics of the day with endemic clarity, biblical knowledge, and insightful presentation of the questions that are in our minds as congregants in the Christian faith. He begins with the questions that have apocalyptic features and refers to the many tragedies in biblical history that might relate to this pandemic. He moves from Old Testament to New Testament, traversing the material of God's relationship to the world and God's compassion. He also grapples with the question of God's sovereignty and love for humanity. He then ends with many practical suggestions for how to move on past this pandemic. It is a useful book to use for an adult class in churches and to share with friends. It is definitely something you should pick up and use for your own edification.

CPSIA information can be obtained
at www.ICGtesting.com
Printed in the USA
FSHW021901270521
81829FS

9 781666 700428